CESSNA 152
Training Manual

By
Oleg Roud and Danielle Bruckert

Red Sky Ventures and Memel CATS
© 2004

Contact the Authors:
We appreciate your feedback.

D Bruckert	O Roud
redskyventures@gmail.com	roudoleg@yahoo.com
+264 81 244 6336	+264 81 208 0566
PO Box 11288 Windhoek, Namibia	PO Box 30421 Windhoek, Namibia
Red Sky Ventures	Memel CATS

Printing and Publication Information

First Edition © 2004 Oleg Roud and Danielle Bruckert
This Edition © 2011 Oleg Roud and Danielle Bruckert

Lulu Paperback Version ISBN 978-0-557-02280-9
Createspace Paperback Version ISBN-13 978-1466234284,
Createspace Paperback Version ISBN-10 1466234288

COPYRIGHT & DISCLAIMER

All rights reserved. No part of this manual may be reproduced for commercial use in any form or by any means without the prior written permission of the authors.

This Training Manual is intended to supplement information you receive from your flight instructor during your type conversion training. It should be used for training and reference only, and is not part of the Civil Aviation Authority or FAA approved Aircraft Operating Manual or Pilot's Operating Handbook. While every effort has been made to ensure completeness and accuracy, should any conflict arise between this training manual and other operating handbooks, the approved aircraft flight manuals or pilot's operating handbook should be used as final reference. Information in this document is subject to change without notice and does not represent a commitment on the part of the authors, nor is it a complete and accurate specification of this product. The authors cannot accept responsibility of any kind from the use of this material.

ACKNOWLEDGEMENTS:

Peter Hartmann, Aviation Center, Windhoek: Supply of technical information, maintenance manuals and CD's for authors research

Brenda Whittaker, Auckland New Zealand: Non Technical Editor

Table of Contents

Introduction..6
   History...6
   Cessna 150...7
   Cessna 152...7
Model History...9
   Models within the Series...9
   Model Versus Serial Number Modifications History.............................10
   Common Modifications 12
      Engine/Propeller Modifications...12
      Tail Wheel 13
      STOL and Speed Kits...13
      Door Latch Modifications..13
Terminology 14
Useful Factors and Formulas..17
   Conversion Factors...17
   Formulas..18
Pilot's Operating Handbook Information...18
AIRCRAFT TECHNICAL INFORMATION..20
   Airframe..21
      Seats and Seat Adjustment..22
      Doors 22
      Baggage Compartment 22
   Flight Controls..24
      Elevator..24
      Rudder...25
      Ailerons..26
      Trim...27
      Flaps..28
   Landing Gear...30
      Shock Absorption..30
      Nose Wheel Construction 31
      Shimmy Damper Construction 32
      Brakes..32
         Park Brake..33
      Towing..34
Engine & Engine Controls...35
   Engine Controls..35
      Throttle..36
      Mixture..36
      Engine Gauges...38
      Tachometer..38
   Induction System and Carb. Heat...39
   Engine Lubrication...40
   Ignition System..41
      Ignition Switch...42
      Dead Cut and Live Mag. Check..42

CESSNA 152 TRAINING MANUAL

Engine Cooling...43
Fuel System...45
   Fuel Measuring and Indication...46
   Priming..46
   Accelerator Pump..47
   Fuel Venting..47
   Fuel Drains..48
   Fuel System Schematic...49
Electrical System...50
   Battery..50
   Alternator..50
   Ground (External) Power Receptacle..51
   Electrical Equipment..51
   System Protection and Distribution...51
   Electrical System Schematic..54
Flight Instruments and Associated Systems..55
   Vacuum System..55
      Vacuum System Schematic..56
   Pitot-Static System 57
   Stall Warning..57
   Accelerometer...58
Ancillary Systems and Equipment...59
   Lighting 59
   Cabin Heating and Ventilating System..59
   Avionics Equipment...60
      Audio Selector..60
      Intercom..61
      VHF Radio Operations 61
      Transponder..61
NORMAL PROCEDURES..62
Pre-flight Check..62
   Cabin...63
   Exterior Inspection..63
   Passenger Brief...68
In-Flight Operations..68
   Before Start...68
      Priming..69
   Start..70
      Flooded Start...70
   After Start...70
   Taxi...71
   Engine Run-up..73
   Pre Takeoff Vital Actions...74
   Takeoff..74
      Wing Flaps Setting on Takeoff...75
      Short Field Takeoff..75
      Soft Field Takeoff..76
      Crosswind Component...76

Crosswind Takeoff	76
Climb	77
Cruise	77
Mixture Setting	77
Cruise Checks	78
Approach and Landing	78
Short Field Landing	79
Crosswind Landing	79
Flapless Landing	80
Balked Landing	80
After Landing Checks	80
Taxi and Shutdown	81
Circuit Pattern	81
Note on Checklists	85
EMERGENCY PROCEDURES	87
Emergency During Takeoff	87
Engine Failure after Takeoff	87
Gliding and Forced Landing	88
Engine Fire	90
Electrical Fire	91
Stalling and Spinning	91
Rough Running Engine	91
Magneto Faults	91
Spark Plug Faults	92
Abnormal Oil Pressure or Temperature	92
Blocked Air Intake	93
Carburettor Ice	93
PERFORMANCE	94
Performance Specifications and Limitations	94
Ground Planning	95
Navigation Planning	95
Fuel Planning	96
Fuel Planning Worksheet	98
Weight and Balance	98
Weight and Balance Calculation	99
Weight & Balance Worksheet	100
Take-off and Landing Performance Planning	101
Takeoff Performance	103
Landing Performance	104
REVIEW QUESTIONS	105

Introduction

This training manual provides a technical and operational descriptions of the the Cessna 152 aeroplane.

The information is intended as an instructional aid to assist with type ratings or ab-initio training and is laid out according to training syllabus for ease of use.
This material does not supersede, nor is it meant to substitute any of the manufacturer's operation manuals. The material presented has been prepared from the basic design data obtained in the pilots operating handbook and from operational experience.

History

The Cessna aircraft company has a long and rich history. Founder Clyde Cessna built his first aeroplane in 1911, and taught himself to fly it!

He went on to build a number of innovative aeroplanes, including several race and award winning designs.

In 1934, Clyde's nephew, Dwane Wallace, fresh out of college, took over as head of the company. During the depression years Dwane acted as everything from floor sweeper to CEO, even personally flying company planes in air races (several of which he won!).

Illustration 1a Cessna 152

Under Wallace's leadership, the Cessna Aircraft Company eventually became the most successful general aviation company of all time.

Cessna first began production of two-seat light planes in 1946 with the model 120 which had an all aluminium fuselage and fabric covered wings.
This was followed by a nearly identical model the 140, with aluminium clad wings.
More than 7,000 model 120-140's were sold over four years when Cessna stopped production in order to focus on four-seat aircraft.

Cessna 150

In 1957 the company decided there was a market for a two seat trainer and designed a tricycle geared version of the Model 140.
Following their standard tailwheel/tricycle model scheme, Cessna named the new aeroplane the 142, but for reasons now unknown changed their minds six days later and renamed it the 150.
Only 683 of the first model were built between 1957 and 1959. All were sold as 1959 models. By 1966 the plane had become enormously popular, over 3000 1966 C150F alone were built, Cessna began assembly in France under contract to Reims Aviation, and in 1967 the first C150 float option was offered.

By the end of production in 1978 there were 23,839 C150's built, including 1764 produced by Reims in France, 47 produced in Argentina under contract to Reims, and a total of 1079 Aerobats.

The Cessna 150 was equipped with a four cylinder 100 horsepower Continental 0-200 engine. During its 18 year production history there were many changes to the C150 design. These changes included increased cabin space, inclusion of the omnivision rear window, improved control surface and cowling design, manual to electric flap, 12 Volt to 24 Volt electrical system, mixture vernier, key starter, and split master switches to name a few. Most of the changes and improvements throughout the C150 development can be considered as contributory to the initial appearance and success of the Cessna 152.

Cessna 152

In 1978 Cessna introduced the new revamped version of the C150, type certified as the C152, with a 110 horsepower Lycoming O-235 engine and modified airframe.
The Lycoming engine was chosen to make the 152 more tolerant of the new 100 octane fuel, as well as provide a long overdue increase in horsepower.
The cabin was widened slightly to make room for the increased girth of late 20th century pilots, and the maximum flap setting was reduced from 40 degrees to 30 degrees for a safer power to drag relationship.

Unlike the C150 model, there were few changes in 152's from one year to the next, and aside from minor technical and trim improvements, the C152 remained outwardly the same throughout the series' production history.

The last Model 152 rolled off the production line in 1985. In it's relatively short 8 year production history, from 1978-1985, there were approximately 7,541 C152's produced worldwide, including 596 assembled by Reims in France, with a total of 396 aerobats.

Because of product liability exposure, Cessna, like most other light plane companies in the US, stopped building light aircraft altogether in the mid 1980's.

Today Cessna is once again in the light aircraft business, building 172's, 182's and 206's. Unfortunately, the high cost of production and insurance premiums make it unlikely that Cessna will reintroduce the Cessna 152. However in 2006, to compete in the light-sports-aircraft (LSA) category, they have unveiled the C162 Skycatcher as the new two seat trainer.

Although we are beginning to see many advances in light aircraft manufacturing, the Cessna 150/152 remains a favourite amongst pilots and flight schools for due to availability, affordability, and the time proven design and handling.

Both the C150 and C152, in all variations, are certified on the same FAA type certificate, No. 3A19.

Model History

The table below summarises the model history versus serial number and significant differences. The information is compiled from the type data certification summaries (TDC) and the technical information in the Cessna maintenance, parts manuals, and operating handbooks.

Models within the Series

All models of C152, those manufactured in Wichita by Cessna, and those manufactured or assembled under contract by Reims, both the aerobat and non aerobat versions are designated by ICAO as a 'C152'. The model designators listed below are the names the manufacturer has given to distinguish the different variants within the type series.

The C152 has only four model variants:
- C152, the Cessna 152 - standard model;
- A152, the Cessna 152 Aerobat, (sometimes called a C152A);
- F152, the Reims Cessna 152;
- FA152, the Reims Cessna 152 Aerobat, (sometimes called a F152A).

There was no deviation in the model designator throughout the years of manufacturer.

Aerobat models all have the following additional features:
- Strengthened main and tail spars and attachments;
- Viewing ports (windows) overhead the pilot/co-pilot seats;
- Quick release cabin doors;
- Full aerobatic harnesses;
- G-meter, and airframe 'g' limits increased to +4, -2;
- Removable seat cushions to facilitate a seat pack or backpack type parachute.

Asides from these additional features, the construction of the Aerobat is the same as the basic model for the respective year.

The C152 II and the C152T are not different models or type variants, but purchase options which were provided with the basic C152.
The C152II had additional avionics for instrument navigation, and additional interior finishes, resulting in a higher basic weight.
The C152T was an options package tailored specifically for sales to flight schools.

Model Versus Serial Number Modifications History

Model	Serial Numbers	Summary of Main Changes
1978		
C152	15279406-15282031	Lycoming O-235-L2C engine rated at 110 HP, 28 volt electrical system, 30 degrees flap, a fuel capacity of 37.5 or 24.5 US gallons usable, McCauley propeller, gross weight 1670 lbs. Aileron droop rigged approximately 1 degree down, commencing serial numbers 15279474, A1520737, F15201429, and FA1520337. Aileron direct and carry through cable turnbuckles shifted from right wing to above headliner, from serial numbers 15281427, A1520786, F1521539, and FA1520353. Beginning with 15279630, F15201529, A1520742, FA1520348,the left hand cap is no longer vented, only the right cap is vented.
F152	F15201449-F15201528	
A152	A1500433, A1520735-A1520808	
FA152	FA1520337-FA1520347	
1979		
C152	15282032-15283591	Minor modifications to instrument panel layout. Exhaust gas temperature (EGT) indicator fitted. Right magneto changed to the Slick 4052 type magneto to match the left, providing impulse couplings on both magnetos to improve starting. Modified engine primer lines for more effective priming. Alternator Voltage Regulator replaced by Alternator Control Unit (ACU), and HIGH VOLTAGE light replaced by a LOW VOLTAGE light. Ignition harness changed from the right magento firing all bottom plugs and left all top plugs, to the right magneto firing bottom right and top left plugs, and the left bottom left and top right plugs, for improved performance and redundancy. Throttle, mixture, and propeller control cable ends changed from ball bearing-type to a pre-drilled bolt, washers castellated nut, and a cotter pin. Light switch added to dome light console and light switch for map light added at door pillar post.Rear view mirror in glareshield removed. Beginning with Aircraft 15283092 on. and A1520853 & on, a Prestolite Slower Turning starter is installed to improve starting characteristics. Clock changed to digital. Brake cylinder redesigned, improving overhaul times. Wheel fairings were not split from 1979, requiring main wheel disassembly for removal, replacements are split.
F152	F15201529-F15201673	
A152	681, A1520809-A1520878	
FA152	FA1520348-FA1520357	

Model	Serial Numbers	Significant Changes and Features
1980		
C152	15283592- 15284541	Accelerator pump incorporated in carburettor. Modified windshield defrosters. Modified battery installation, eliminating battery box. Carb. heat source changed from the muffler to a shroud at #4 cylinder, beginning with15284899, F15201894, A1520971 and FA1520378. Simulated wood instrument panels introduced. Magneto changed from Slick 4052 to Slick 42181 at serial numbers 15284028 and A1520915.
F152	F15201674- F15201808	
A152	A1520879- A1520948	
FA152	FA1520358- FA1520372	
1981		
C152	15284542- 15285161	Spin-on oil filter now standard. Larger capacity battery contactor to reduce 'welding' occurrences. Integral intercom standard in trainer purchase options (C152T), optional on other versions. Avionics cooling fan introduced. Modified vertical fin and horizontal stabilizer attachment. Modified vacuum system. Modified bus bar. Cabin door latch system altered at serial numbers 15284730 and A1520961 to include a ball and spring plate. Interior vents changed at serial numbers 15284924, F15201894, A1520972, and FA1520378, to provide better access and more air supply.
F152	F15201809- F15201893	
A152	A1520949- A1520983	
FA152	FA1520373- FA1520377	
1982		
C152	15285162- 15285594	Additional fuel quick drain in belly below fuel selector. White toggle switches for avionics equipment introduced. On models with optional navigational equipment, the "Bow-tie" glideslope antenna was eliminated, and an antenna coupler is utilized to allow the nav receiver to receive glideslope signals. Wing root air vents are made smaller to allow for better sealing.
F152	F15201894- F15201928	
A152	A1520984- A1521014	
FA152	FA1520378- FA1520382	
1983		
C152	15285595- 15285833	Engine changed to Lycoming O-235-N2C, 108 HP to address lead fouling problems.

Model	Serial Numbers	Significant Changes and Features
F152	F15201929-F15201943	Avionics cooling fan improved. Vacuum system includes low-vacuum warning light. Gyro instrument installation redesigned to allow removal of gyro instruments from the front of the panel.
A152	A1521015-A1521025	
FA152	FA1520383-FA1520387	
1984		
C152	15285834-15285939	Landing and taxi light wing mounted.
F152	F15201944-F15201952	
A152	A1521026-A1521027	
1985		
C152	15285940-15286033	Aileron hinge changed at serial number 1525916 and A1521028.
F152	F15201953-F15201965	
A152	A1521028-A1521049	
FA152	FA1520388-FA1520415	
FA152	FA1520416-FA1520425	These serial numbers are listed by the manufacturer as produced in 1986, however all type certifiation information refer to production ceasing in 1985. It can be assumed no changes were made and the models were registered as 1985 builds.

Common Modifications

There are a large number of Supplemental Type Certificates issued by the FAA for modifications to the C152. The following lists some of the more commonly found.

Engine/Propeller Modifications

The 'Sparrowhawk' 125hp engine with Sensenich propeller is available from AirMods Inc. The installation includes a top overhaul, that is, larger pistons, and a modified propeller and spinner. The modifications can be done together or separately, as the engine and propeller upgrades are much more economic if completed with the routine overhaul schedules on each. The Sensenich propeller comes in three pitch options, which are an important consideration, as a climb pitch will disappoint someone upgrading for speed, and likewise a cruise pitch, even with the higher horsepower may perform worse than a standard installation in the climb.

Lycoming O320 and O360 engine installations are available, providing increases in power to 150hp or 180hp, O&N Aircraft Technologies has one of the most popular options for this upgrade.
Note, on non-aerobat models, engine upgrades may impose restrictions on spinning because of the modified lift-weight couple. This may be of importance if looking at purchasing an aircraft or installing the upgrade for use in a flight school.

Tail Wheel
It is possible to convert the tricycle landing gear to a tail wheel version, providing shorter landing and takeoff distances and the more streamlined profile improves cruise speed. Many existing examples of this conversion can be found.
A tailwheel conversion involves strengthening of the fuselage and tail area for the new gear positions, removal of the nose wheel, alteration of the main gear, and addition of the tail wheel.
One of the most popular tail wheel conversions fitted to the C152 is the Texas Taildragger kit, from Aircraft Conversion Technologies, although they are no longer in operation which may cause problems with maintenance on existing installations. Tail wheel conversions are also available from Bush Conversions.

STOL and Speed Kits
Various STOL and speed kits are available, including the wing tip modifications, leading edge modifications, flap gaps seals, vortex generator (VG) kits, fairing and cowl modifications, and wing fences. One of the more common STOL kits is the Horton STOL, including wing tip fences, leading edge modifications and drooping wing tips, all acting to reduce stall speed, and reducing takeoff and landing speeds and thus distances.

Door Latch Modifications
Many door catch modifications are available to replace the pull to close type which often fail with wear resulting in poor closing and latching.
Note, door latch modifications that lock may not be applicable to Aerobats since they can operate in conflict with the quick release door hinges.

Fuel Modifications
Various fuel system modifications are available, including conversions to auto-fuel, auxiliary fuel tanks, additional sump (belly) drains and modified gascolators for removing water from the fuel system.
One of the most common auxiliary fuel tank modification is available from O&N Aircraft Modifications, providing 14 US gallons additional fuel, and featuring a baggage compartment tank with a transfer pump connected to the right wing.
The Texas Ranger Fuel Tanks from Aircraft Conversion Technologies provide an additional 7USG per tank.

Terminology

Airspeed		
KIAS	Knots Indicated Airspeed	Speed in knots as indicated on the airspeed indicator.
KCAS	Knots Calibrated Airspeed	KIAS corrected for instrument error. Note this error is often negligible and CAS may be omitted from calculations.
KTAS	Knots True Airspeed	KCAS corrected for density (altitude and temperature) error.
Va	Max Manoeuvering Speed	The maximum speed for full or abrupt control inputs.
Vfe	Maximum Flap Extended Speed	The highest speed permitted with flap extended. Indicated by the top of the white arc.
Vno	Maximum Structural Cruising Speed	Sometimes referred to as "normal operating range". Should not be exceeded except in smooth conditions and only with caution. Indicated by the green arc.
Vne	Never Exceed speed	Maximum speed permitted, exceeding will cause structural damage. Indicated by the upper red line.
Vs	Stall Speed	The minimum speed before loss of control in the normal cruise configuration. Indicated by the bottom of the green arc. Sometimes referred to as minimum 'steady flight' speed.
Vso	Stall Speed Landing Configuration	The minimum speed before loss of control in the landing configuration, at the most forward C of G*. Indicated by the bottom of the white arc.
*forward centre of gravity gives a higher stall speed and so is used for certification		
Vx	Best Angle of Climb Speed	The speed which results in the maximum gain in altitude for a given horizontal distance.
Vy	Best Rate of Climb Speed	The speed which results in the maximum gain in altitude for a given time, indicated by the maximum rate of climb for the conditions on the VSI.
Vref	Reference Speed	The minimum safe approach speed, calculated as 1.3 x Vso.
Vbug	Nominated Speed	The speed nominated as indicated by the speed bug, for approach this is Vref plus a safety margin for conditions.

Vr	Rotation Speed	The speed which rotation should be initiated.
Vat	Barrier Speed	The speed to maintain at the 50ft barrier or on reaching 50ft above the runway.
	Maximum Demonstrated Crosswind	The maximum demonstrated crosswind during testing.

Meteorological Terms

OAT	Outside Air Temperature	Free outside air temperature, or indicated outside air temperature corrected for gauge, position and ram air errors.
IOAT	Indicated Outside Air Temperature	Temperature indicated on the temperature gauge.
ISA	International Standard Atmosphere	The ICAO international atmosphere, as defined in document 7488. Approximate conditions are a sea level temperature of 15 degrees with a lapse rate of 1.98 degrees per 1000ft, and a sea level pressure of 1013mb with a lapse rate of 1mb per 30ft.
	Standard Temperature	The temperature in the International Standard atmosphere for the associated level, and is 15 degrees Celsius at sea level decreased by two degrees every 1000ft.
	Pressure Altitude	The altitude in the International Standard Atmosphere with a sea level pressure of 1013 and a standard reduction of 1mb per 30ft. Pressure Altitude would be observed with the altimeter subscale set to 1013.
	Density Altitude	The altitude that the prevailing density would occur in the International Standard Atmosphere, and can be found by correcting Pressure Altitude for temperature deviations.

Engine Terms

BHP	Brake Horse Power	The power developed by the engine (actual power available will have some transmission losses).
RPM	Revolutions per Minute	Engine drive and propeller speed.
	Static RPM	The maximum RPM obtained during stationery full throttle operation

Weight and Balance Terms

	Moment Arm	The horizontal distance in inches from reference datum line to the centre of gravity of the item concerned, or from the datum to the item 'station'.
C of G	**Centre of Gravity**	The point about which an aeroplane would balance if it were possible to suspend it at that point. It is the mass centre of the aeroplane, or the theoretical point at which entire weight of the aeroplane is assumed to be concentrated. It may be expressed in percent of MAC (mean aerodynamic chord) or in inches from the reference datum.
	Centre of Gravity Limit	The specified forward and aft points beyond which the CG must not be located. Typically, the forward limit primarily effects the controllability of aircraft and aft limits stability of the aircraft.
	Datum (reference datum)	An imaginary vertical plane or line from which all measurements of arm are taken. The datum is established by the manufacturer.
	Moment	The product of the weight of an item multiplied by its arm and expressed in inch-pounds. The total moment is the weight of the aeroplane multiplied by distance between the datum and the CG.
MZFW	**Maximum Zero Fuel Weight**	The maximum permissible weight to prevent exceeding the wing bending limits. This limit is not always applicable for aircraft with small fuel loads.
BEW	**Basic Empty Weight**	The weight of an empty aeroplane, including permanently installed equipment, fixed ballast, full oil and unusable fuel, and is that specified on the aircraft mass and balance documentation for each individual aircraft.
SEW	**Standard Empty Weight**	The basic empty weight of a standard aeroplane, specified in the POH, and is an average weight given for performance considerations and calculations.
OEW	**Operating Empty Weight**	The weight of the aircraft with crew, unusable fuel, and operational items (galley etc.).
	Payload	The weight the aircraft can carry with the pilot and fuel on board.
MRW	**Maximum Ramp Weight**	The maximum weight for ramp manoeuvring, the maximum takeoff weight plus additional fuel for start taxi and runup.

MTOW	Maximum Takeoff Weight	The maximum permissible takeoff weight and sometimes called the maximum all up weight, landing weight is normally lower as allows for burn off and carries shock loads on touchdown.
MLW	Maximum Landing Weight	Maximum permissible weight for landing. Sometimes this is the same as the takeoff weight for smaller aircraft.
Note: The correct technical is 'mass' instead of 'weight' in all of these terms, however in everyday language and in many aircraft operating manuals the term weight remains in common use. In this context there is no difference in meaning and the terms may be interchanged.		
Other		
AFM	Aircraft Flight Manual	These terms are inter-changeable and refer to the approved manufacturer's handbook. General Aviation manufacturers from 1976 began using the term 'Pilot's Operating Handbook', early manuals were called Owner's Manual and most legal texts use the term AFM.
POH	Pilot's Operating Handbook	
PIM	Pilot Information Manual	A Pilot Information Manual is a new term, coined to refer to a POH or AFM which is not issued to a specific aircraft

Useful Factors and Formulas

Conversion Factors

Lbs to kg	1kg =2.204lbs	kgs to lbs	1lb = .454kgs
USG to Lt	1USG = 3.785Lt	lt to USG	1lt = 0.264USG
Lt to Imp Gal	1lt = 0.22 Imp G	Imp.Gal to lt	1Imp G = 4.55lt
NM to KM	1nm = 1.852km	km to nm	1km = 0.54nm
NM to StM to ft	1nm = 1.15stm 1nm = 6080ft	Stm to nm to ft	1 stm = 0.87nm 5280ft
FT to Meters	1 FT = 0.3048 m	meters to ft	1 m = 3.281 FT
Inches to Cm	1 inch = 2.54cm	cm to inches	1cm = 0.394"
Hpa(mb) to "Hg	1mb = .029536"	" Hg to Hpa (mb)	1" = 33.8mb

by D. Bruckert & O. Roud © 2004

AVGAS FUEL Volume / Weight SG = 0.72						
Litres	Lt/kg	kgs	Litres	lbs/lts	Lbs
1.39	1	0.72	0.631	1	1.58

Crosswind Component per 10kts of Wind							
Deg	10	20	30	40	50	60	70	80
Kts	2	3	5	6	8	9	9	10

Formulas

Celsius (C) to Fahrenheit (F)	C = 5/9 x(F-32),
	F = Cx9/5+32
Pressure altitude (PA)	PA = Altitude AMSL + 30 x (1013-QNH)
	Memory aid – Subscale up/down altitude up/down
Standard Temperature (ST)	ST = 15 – 2 x PA/1000
	ie. 2 degrees cooler per 1000ft altitude
Density altitude (DA)	DA = PA +(-) 120ft/deg above (below) ST
	i.e. 120ft higher for every degree hotter than standard
Specific Gravity	SG x volume in litres = weight in kgs
One in 60 rule	1 degree of arc ≈ 1nm at a radius of 60nm
	i.e degrees of arc approximately equal length of arc at a radius of 60nm
Rate 1 Turn Radius	R = TAS per hour/60/π or TAS per minute/π
	R ≈ TAS per hour/180 (Where π (pi) ≈3.14)
Radius of Turn Rule of Thumb	Radius of Turn lead allowance ≈ 1% of ground speed
	(This rule can be used for turning on to an arc – eg at 100kts GS, start turn 1nm before the arc limit)
Rate 1 Turn Bank Angle Rule of Thumb	degrees of bank in a rate one turn ≈ GS/10+7

Pilot's Operating Handbook Information

The approved manufacturer's handbook, normally termed Pilot's Operating Handbook (POH) or Aircraft Flight Manual (AFM),or owners manual, is issued for the specific model and serial number, and includes all applicable supplements and modifications. It is legally required to be on board the aircraft during flight, and is the master document for all flight information.

In 1975, the US General Aviation Manufacturer's Association introduced the 'GAMA Specification No. 1' format for the 'Pilot's Operating Handbook' (POH). This format was later adopted by ICAO in their Guidance Document 9516 in 1991, and is now required for all newly certified aircraft by ICAO member states. Most light aircraft listed as built in 1976 or later, have provided Pilot's Operating Handbooks (POHs) in this format.

This format was designed to enhance safety by not only standardising layouts but sldo considering ergonomic use in flight. It is therefore recommended that pilots become familiar with the order and contents of each section, as summarised in the table below.

Section 1	General	Definitions and abbreviations
Section 2	Limitations	Specific operating limits, placards and specifications
Section 3	Emergencies	Complete descriptions of action in the event of any emergency or non-normal situation
Section 4	Normal Operations	Complete descriptions of required actions for all normal situations
Section 5	Performance	Performance graphs, typically for stall speeds, airspeed calibration, cross wind calculation, takeoff, climb, cruise, and landing
Section 6	Weight and Balance	Loading specifications, limitations and loading graphs or tables
Section 7	Systems Descriptions	Technical descriptions of aircraft systems, airframe, controls, fuel, engine, instruments, avionics and lights etc.
Section 8	Servicing and maintenance	Maintenance requirements, inspections, stowing, oil requirements etc.
Section 9	Supplements	Supplement sections follow the format above for additional equipment or modification.
Section 10	Safety Information	General safety information and helpful operational recommendations which the manufacturer feels are pertinent to the operation of the aircraft

For use in ground training, or reference prior to flight, this text should be read in conjunction with the POH from on board the aircraft you are going to be flying. Even if you have a copy of a POH for the same model C182, the aircraft you are flying may have supplements for modifications and optional equipment which affect the operational performance.

AIRCRAFT TECHNICAL INFORMATION

The Cessna 152 aeroplane is a single engine, two-seat, high-wing monoplane aircraft, equipped with tricycle landing gear and designed for general utility purposes.

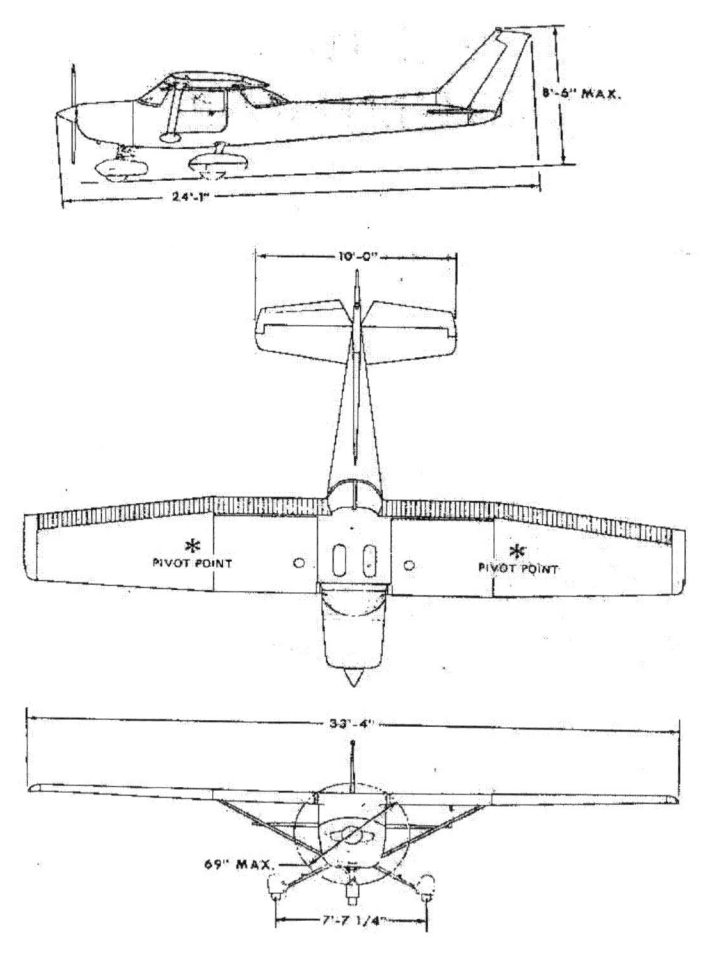

Illustration 2a Cessna 152 Profiles

Airframe

The airframe is a conventional semi-monocoque type consisting of formed sheet metal bulkheads, stringers and stressed skin.

Semi-monocoque construction is a light framework covered by skin that carries much of the stress. It is a combination of the best features of a strut-type structure, in which the internal framework carries almost all of the stress, and the pure monocoque where all stress is carried by the skin.

The fuselage forms the main body of the aircraft to which the wings, tail section and undercarriage are attached. The main structural features are:
- ✈ front and rear carry through spars for wing attachment;
- ✈ a bulkhead and forgings for landing gear attachment;
- ✈ a bulkhead and attaching plates for strut mounting;
- ✈ four stringers for engine mounting attached to the forward door posts.

The wings are all metal, semi-cantilever type with a struts spanning the inner section of the wing. They contain the integral ie. non bladder type fuel tanks.

The empennage or tail assembly consists of the vertical stabilizer and rudder, horizontal stabilizer and elevator.

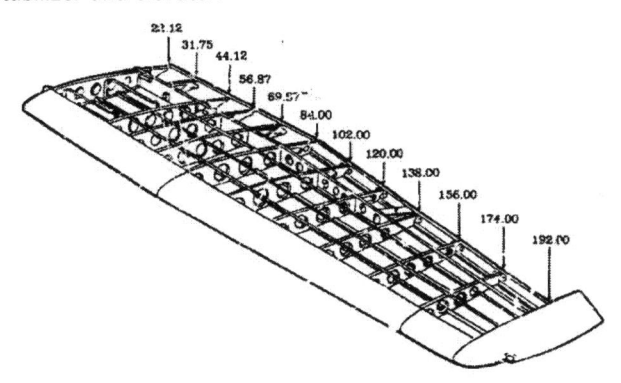

Illustration 2b Wing Construction

The construction of the wing and empennage sections consists of:
- ✈ a front (vertical stabilizer) or front and rear spar (wings/horizontal stabilizer);
- ✈ formed sheet metal ribs;
- ✈ doublers and stringers;
- ✈ wrap around and formed sheet metal/aluminium skin panels;
- ✈ control surfaces, flap and trim assembly and associated linkages.

Seats and Seat Adjustment

The seating arrangement consists of two separate adjustable seats for the pilot and co-pilot or front passenger, and an optional auxiliary child's seat (if installed) aft of the front seats.

The pilot and copilot seats are adjustable in forward and aft position, and for seat height and back inclination. Seat back and height should be adjusted to ensure adequate visibility and control *before* start-up.

When adjusting the seats forward and aft care should be taken to ensure the position is locked. Seat locks are available and installed on many aircraft following accidents involving slipping of seat position during critical phases of flight.

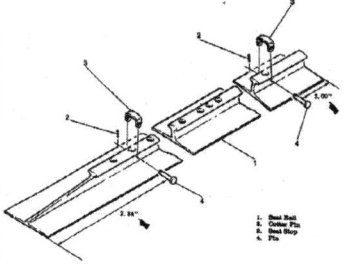

Illustration 2C Seat Rail

To ensure the seat is secure, the vertical pin attached to the seat must be firmly positioned down in the seat rail holes (displayed in the picture above). Ensure the seat is secure by applying pressure forwards and backwards to ensure it will not come loose from the rail during movement.

During pre-flight, the seat rail, mountings and mounting pin should be checked for integrity. The rails are prone to cracking around the weak points created by the locking and fastening holes, the locking pin may be loose or the spring worn, and the rails can sometimes come loose, without the pilot being aware, when the seat is moved too far forward or aft.

Doors

There are two entrance doors provided, one on the left and one on the fight, and a baggage door at the rear left side of the aircraft.

The door latch is a pull to close, quick release type latch, and can only be locked from the outside.

Some aircraft may have a modified interior door latch installed to enable locking the door from the inside, various modifications are available.

Baggage Compartment

The baggage compartment consists of the area from the back of the rear passenger seats to the aft cabin bulkhead. A baggage shelf, above the wheel well, extends aft from the aft cabin bulkhead. Access to the baggage compartment and the shelf is gained through a lockable baggage door on the left side of the airplane, or from within the airplane cabin.

When loading the airplane, children should not be placed or permitted in the baggage compartment, unless an approved auxiliary child seat is installed.

Any material that may be hazardous to the airplane or occupants should never be placed anywhere in the aircraft. This includes items such as petrol ferry tanks, lead acid batteries, common household solvents such as paint thinners and many more. Items such as these can cause life threatening consequences from incapacitation due to exposure to leaking fumes, cabin fire caused by spillage combined with a static spark, explosion under pressure changes, or result in serious corrosion damage to the airframe. If any doubt exists, consult the IATA guidelines for permitted quantities of dangerous goods.

When using an approved auxiliary child seat, it is important to ensure that loading is completed within the aircraft limits, for the maximum mass and the position of the centre of gravity. More details on loading are provided in the Performance Section.

Flight Controls

The aeroplane's flight control system consists of conventional aileron, rudder and elevator control surfaces. The control surfaces are manually operated through mechanical linkages to the control wheel for the ailerons and elevator, and rudder/brake pedals for the rudder. A manually-operated elevator trim tab is provided and installed on the right elevator.

The control surfaces are formed in a similar way to the wing and tail section with the inclusion of the balance weights, actuation system (control cables etc) and trim tabs. Control actuation is provided by a series of push-pull rods, bellcranks, pulleys and cables with the required individual connections.

Elevator

The elevator is hinged to the rear part of the horizontal stabilizer on both sides. The main features are:
- ✈ an inset hinge with balance weights;
- ✈ an adjustable trim tab on the right side.

The leading edge of both left and right elevator tips incorporate extensions which contain the balance weights which aerodynamically and mechanically assists with control input reducing the force required to move the control.

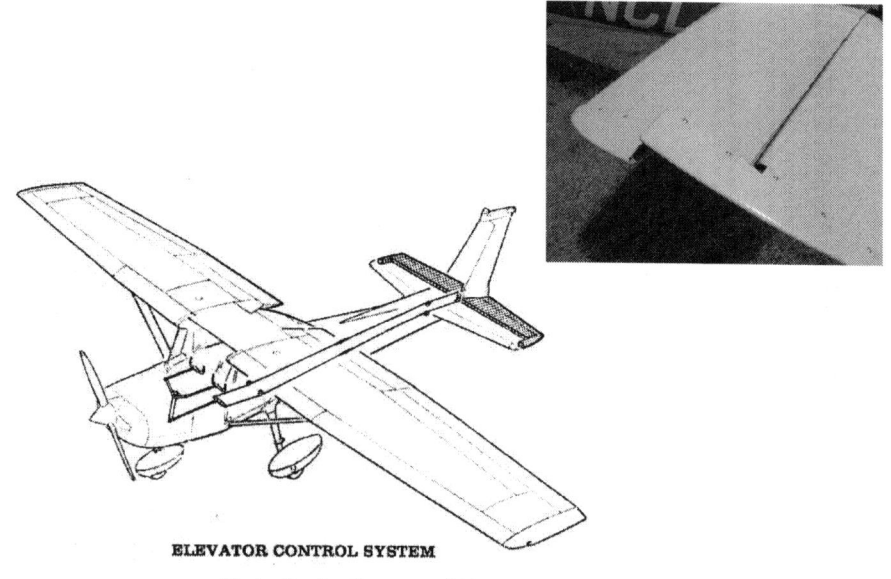

Illustration 3a Elevator and Elevator Control Connections

Rudder

The rudder forms the aft part of the vertical stabilizer. The main features include
- ✈ a ground adjustable trim tab at the base;
- ✈ horn balance tab and balance weight.

The top of the rudder incorporates a leading edge extension which contains a balance weight and aerodynamically assists with control input in the same way as the elevator hinge point. The rudder movement is limited by stop at 23 degrees either side of neutral. The rudder linkage is additionally connected to the nose wheel steering to assist with ground control.

The fixed rudder trim tab, on the lower rear edge of the rudder, is delicate and care should be taken not to mishandle the tab when checking the rudder serviceability.

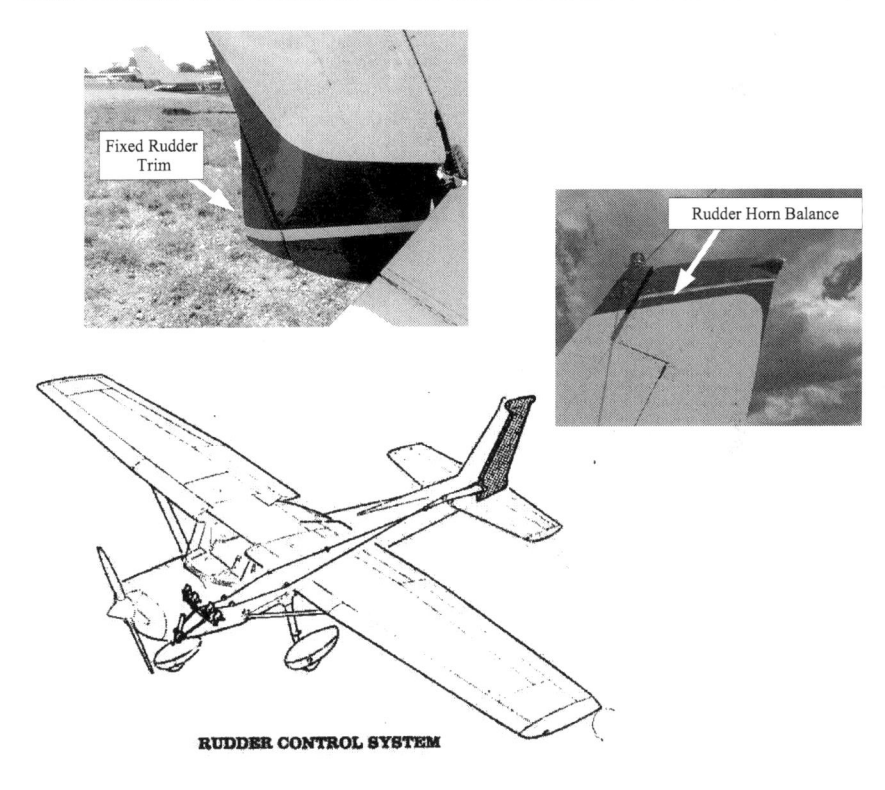

Illustration 3b Rudder and Rudder Control Connections

Ailerons

Conventional hinged ailerons are attached to the trailing edge of the wings. Main features of the aileron design include:
- ✈ a forward spar containing aerodynamic "anti-flutter" balance weights;
- ✈ "V" type corrugated aluminum skin joined together at the trailing edge;
- ✈ differential and Frise design.

Differential and Frise Ailerons

The ailerons include Differential and Frise design. Differential refers to the larger angle of travel in the up position to the down position, increasing drag on the down-going wing. Frise-Type ailerons are constructed so that the forward part of the up-going aileron protrudes into the air stream below the wing to increase the drag on the down-going wing. Both features acting to reduce the effect of Adverse Aileron Yaw, reducing the required rudder input during balanced turns. These features have the additional advantage of assisting with aerodynamic balancing of the ailerons.

The ailerons control system additionally includes:
- ✈ sprockets and roller chains;
- ✈ a control "Y" which interconnects the control wheel to the aileron cables.

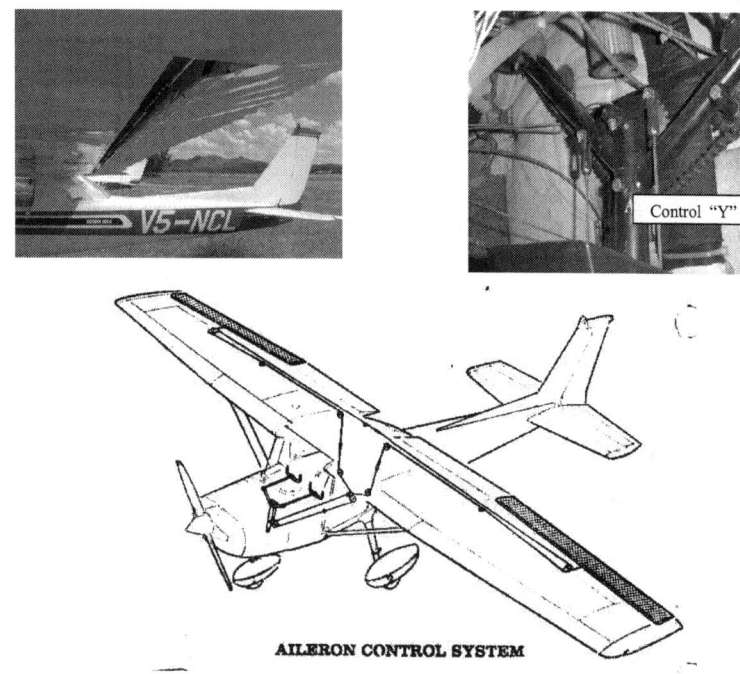

Illustration 3c Aileron and Aileron Control Conections

Trim

One trim tab is provided on the right side of the elevator, spanning most of the the rear section of the right elevator. The trim tab moves opposite to the control surface, reducing the aerodynamic force on the control surface in order to hold the selected position.

Trimming is accomplished through the elevator trim tab by turning the vertically mounted trim control wheel. Forward (up) rotation of the trim wheel will trim nose-down, conversely, aft (down) rotation will trim nose-up.

ELEVATOR TRIM CONTROL SYSTEM

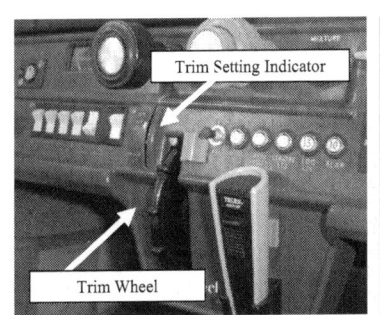

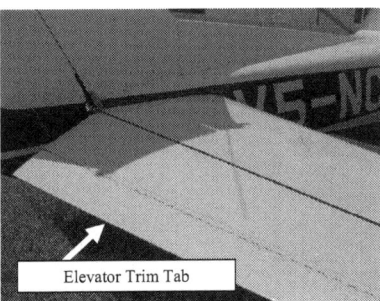

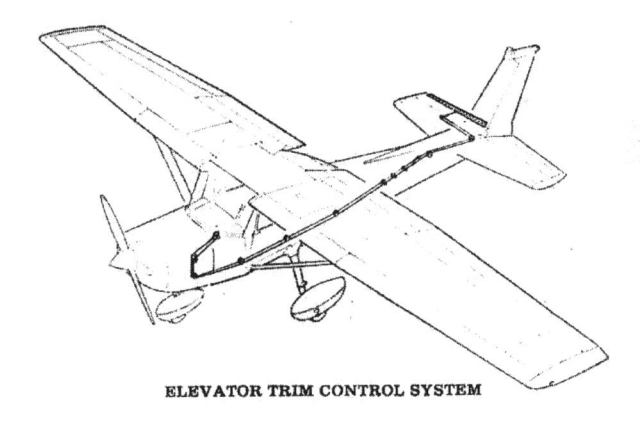

Illustration 3d Elevator Trim, Trim Control and Connections

Flaps

The flaps are constructed basically the same as the ailerons with the exception of the balance weights and the addition of a formed sheet metal leading edge section.

The maximum deflection of the flaps is 30 degrees. All models have electrical flap with a pre-select type flap lever.

The wing flaps are of the single-slot, Fowler type. Both design features act to further reduce the stalling speed.
The single slot modifies the direction of the airflow to maintain laminar flow longer.
The fowler design increasing the size of the wing surface area on extension.

The wings flap control system is comprised of:
- ✈ an electronic motor;
- ✈ transmission assembly;
- ✈ drive pulley, cables, and push-pull rods;
- ✈ follow-up control.

Power from the motor and transmission assembly is transmitted to the flaps by the drive pulley, cables and push-pull rods.

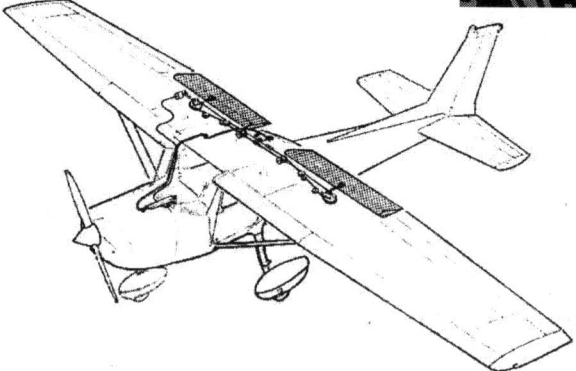

Slotted Fowler Flap

Wing Flap System

Illustration 3e Flaps and Flap Connections

Electrical power to the motor is controlled by two microswitches mounted on a floating arm assembly, through a camming lever and follow-up control. They are extended or retracted by positioning the flap lever on the instrument panel to the desired flap deflection position.

The switch lever is moved up or down in a slot in the instrument panel that provides mechanical stops at the 10 and 20 degree positions. For settings greater than 10 degrees, move the switch level to the right to clear the stop and position it as desired. A scale and pointer on the left side of the switch level indicates flap travel in degrees.

The flap system is protected by a 15-ampere circuit breaker, labeled FLAP, on the right side of the instrument panel.

When the flap control lever is moved to the desired flap setting, an attached cam trips one of the microswitches, activating the flap motor. As the flaps move to the position selected, the floating arm is rotated by the follow-up control until the active microswitch clears the cam, breaking the circuits and stopping the motor. To reverse flap direction the control lever is moved in the opposite direction causing the cam to trip a second microswitch which reverses the flap motor.
The follow-up control moves the cam until it is clear of the second switch, shutting off the flap motor. Failure of a microswitch will render the system inoperative without indication as to why.
Limit switches on flap actuator assembly prevent over-travel of the flaps in the full UP or DOWN positions. Failure of limit switches will cause the motor to continue to run after the desired position is reached.

Illustration 3f Flap Selector

Landing Gear

The landing gear is of the tricycle type with a steerable nose wheel and two fixed main wheels. The landing gear may be equipped with wheel fairings for reducing drag.

The steerable nose wheel is mounted on a forked bracket attached to an air/oil (oleo) shock strut. The shock strut is secured to the tubular engine mount.

Nose wheel steering is accomplished by two spring-loaded steering bungees linking the nose gear steering collar to the rudder pedal bars. Steering is afforded up to 8.5 degrees each side of neutral, after which brakes may be used to gain a maximum deflection of 30 degrees right or left of center. During flight the nose wheel leg extends fully, bringing a locking mechanism into place which holds the nose wheel central and free from rudder pedal action.

Shock Absorption

Shock absorption on the main gear is provided by the tabular spring-steel main landing gear struts and air/oil nose gear shock strut, commonly known as the "oleo". Because of this the main gear is far more durable than the nose gear and is thus intended for the full absorption of the landing.

Illustration 4a Nose Wheel Components

Correct extension of shock strut is important to proper landing gear operation. Too little extension will mean no shock absorption resulting in shock damage during taxi and landing. Too much extension will result in difficult nose wheel steering and premature nose wheel contact on landing may occur. Should the strut extend fully while on the ground the locking mechanism will cause a complete loss of nose wheel steering. During the pre-flight inspection, check the shock strut for proper extension, (approximately two inches or five centimetres), and check the shock absorption properties (lift the nose of the aircraft and release to ensure a firm but resonant feel).

A hydraulic fluid-filled shimmy damper is provided to minimize nose wheel shimmy. The shimmy damper offers resistance to shimmy (nose wheel oscillation) by forcing hydraulic fluid through small orifices in a piston. The dampener piston shaft is secured to a stationary part and the housing is secured to the nose wheel steering collar which moves as the nose wheel is turned right or left, causing relative motion between the dampener shaft and housing. This movement in turn provides the resistance to the small vibrations of the nose wheel.

Nose Wheel Construction

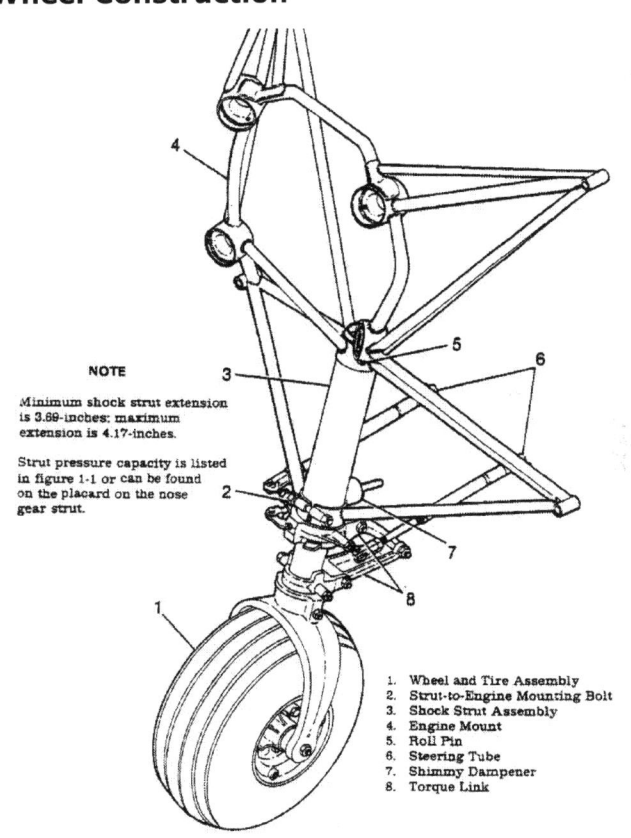

NOTE

Minimum shock strut extension is 3.89-inches; maximum extension is 4.17-inches.

Strut pressure capacity is listed in figure 1-1 or can be found on the placard on the nose gear strut.

1. Wheel and Tire Assembly
2. Strut-to-Engine Mounting Bolt
3. Shock Strut Assembly
4. Engine Mount
5. Roll Pin
6. Steering Tube
7. Shimmy Dampener
8. Torque Link

Illustration 4b Nose Wheel Construction

Shimmy Damper Construction

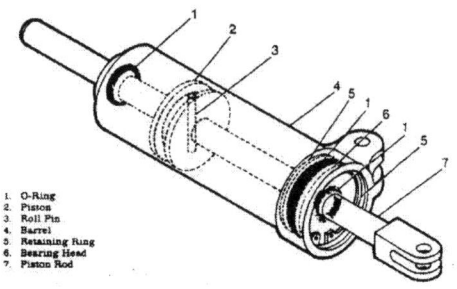

Illustration 4c Shimmy Damper

1. O-Ring
2. Piston
3. Roll Pin
4. Barrel
5. Retaining Ring
6. Bearing Head
7. Piston Rod

Brakes

Each main gear wheel is equipped with a hydraulically actuated disc-type brake on the inboard side of each wheel. When wheel fairings are installed the aerodynamic fairing covers each brake.

The hydraulic brake system is comprised of:
- two master cylinders immediately forward of the pilot's rudder pedals;
- a brake line and hose connecting each master cylinder to its wheel brake cylinder;
- a single-disc, floating cylinder-type brake assembly on each main wheel
- A parking brake control.

Illustration 4d Brake Components

The brake master cylinders located immediately forward of the pilot's rudder pedals, are actuated by applying pressure at the top of the rudder pedals. A small reservoir is incorporated into each master cylinder for the fluid supply. Mechanical linkage permits the co-pilot (instructor) pedals to operate the master cylinders.

Through their operation it is easily possible to inadvertently use brakes whilst under power. This increases war on brakes and increases stopping distances. Prior to applying brakes to stop the aircraft always ensure the throttle is closed.

Park Brake

The park brake system consists of a control knob on the instrument panel which is connected to linkage at the brake master cylinders. At the brake master cylinders, the control operates locking plates which trap pressure in the system after the master cylinder piston rods have been depressed by toe operation of the rudder pedals.

The method of using the parking brake system is:
1. Apply pressure on the top of the rudder pedals;
2. Pull parking brake control to the out position;
3. Release toe pressure;
4. Release park brake control.

Illustration 4e Park Brake Control

To release the parking brake, depress the pedals and ensure the control knob is full in. The park brake should be released when securing the aircraft after installing chocks to prevent locking.

🕮The control knob parking brake is much less intuitive than the handle type, and more prone to sticking, and pilot's who are used to the handle typ of parking brake should be aware of the potential hazards.

Towing

Moving the aircraft by hand is best accomplished by using the wing struts and landing gear struts as a push point. A tow bar attached to the nose gear should be used for steering and manoeuvering the aircraft on the ground. When towing the aircraft, never turn the nose wheel more then 30 degrees either side of center or the nose gear will be damaged.

When no tow bar is available, the aircraft may be manoeuvered by pressing down on the tail section, to raise the nose wheel and and then sideways towards the desired change of direction.

Ensure to press down on the rear section of the main fuselage immediately forward of the vertical stabilizer leading edge. DO NOT to press on the control surfaces or horizontal/vertical stabilizers as structural damage will occur to the mounting or skin surface.

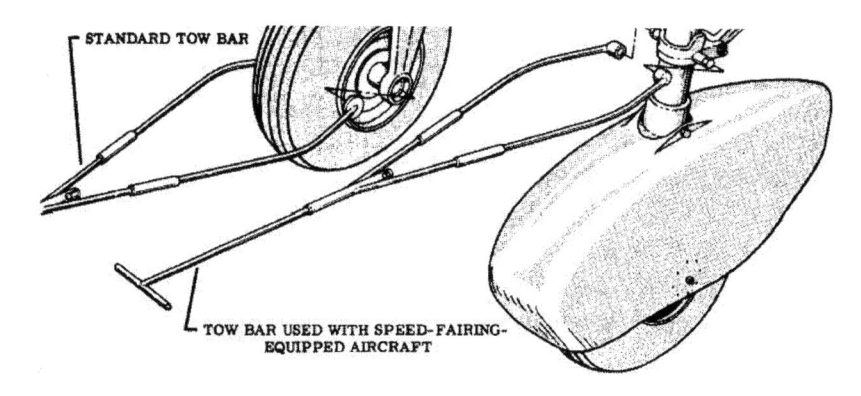

Illustration 4f Towbar Configurations

Engine & Engine Controls

The engine installation on the Cessna 152 is a four cylinder horizontally opposed, air-cooled, carburettor engine.

The engine installation is:
- → Prior to 1983 a Lycoming O-235-L2C, developing 110 horsepower at 2550 rpm at sea level;
- → 1983 and later a Lycoming O-235-N2C, developing 108 horsepower at 2550 rpm at sea level.

The total time before overhaul (TBO) recommended by Avco Lycoming for the 235 series is either 2000 or 2400 hours depending on the engine and engine components fitted.

The Cessna 152 is equipped with a two-bladed, fixed pitch, aluminum alloy propeller. The propeller is approximately 1.75 metres (69 inches) in diameter, with a static rpm of 2280 to 2380rpm.

Illustration 5a Engine Installation

Engine Controls

The engine control and monitoring consists of:
- → Throttle Control;
- → Mixture Control;
- → Carb. Heat selector;
- → Engine monitoring gauges;
  - Tachometer;
  - Oil temperature and pressure;
  - Exhaust Gas Temperature (1979 models on);
  - Cylinder Head Temperature (optional).

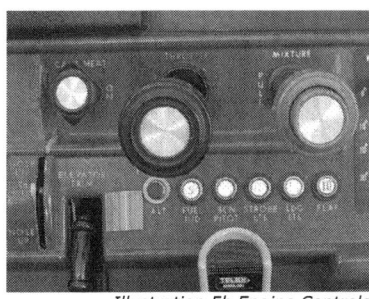

Illustration 5b Engine Controls

Throttle

Engine power is controlled by a throttle, located on the lower center portion of the instrument panel.

The throttle controls a throttle valve (or butterfly) – an oval metal disc pivoted on a central spindle that is perpendicular to the axis of the carburettor's manifold. The closed position of the valve is when the disc is rotated to an angle of about 70° to the axis of the manifold, preventing all but enough fuel/air for idling to pass through the manifold. When the valve is rotated to a position parallel to the axis of the manifold it offers very little restriction to airflow. This is the fully open position of the valve providing maximum fuel/air mixture to the manifold.

The throttle control operates in a conventional manner:
- **full forward** position, the throttle is **open** and the engine produces **maximum** power;
- **full aft** position, it is **closed** and the engine is **idling** or windmilling.

The picture below shows open and closed positions of the throttle butterfly.

Throttle in Open Position   **Throttle in Closed Position**

Illustration 5c Throttle Butterfly

Throttle Friction Nut

A friction lock, which is a round knurled disk, is located at the base of the throttle and is operated by rotating the lock clockwise to increase friction or counterclockwise to decrease it. This allows for reducing friction for smooth operations when frequent or large power changes are required or increasing friction when a fixed power setting or minimum changes are required.

Mixture

The mixture control is a red vernier type control for adjusting fuel/air ratio.

The mixture is used in the conventional way as follows:
- **full forward** position is the **fully rich** position (maximum fuel to air ratio);
- **full aft** position is the **idle cut-off** position (no fuel).

For fine adjustments, the control may be moved forward by rotating the vernier knob clockwise (enriching the mixture), and aft by rotating it counterclockwise (leaning the mixture). For rapid or large adjustments, the control may be moved forward or aft by depressing the lock button on the end of the control, and then positioning the control as desired. When setting in flight the vernier should always be used.

The mixture control should be set to "full rich" for take-off below 3,000 feet of **density** altitude. Above 3,000 feet it is recommended the mixture be leaned to the correct setting before take-off.

Mixture Setting

For carburettor engines, to provide adequate cooling and prevent detonation, the mixture setting should always be slightly rich of the maximum power setting or "peak rpm", to allow for variations between cylinders. This is achieved by rotating the mixture counterclockwise until maximum rpm is obtained with a fixed throttle setting, where on further leaning the rpm begins to decrease, accompanied by slight rough running as cylinders begin to misfire. Then the control is rotated clockwise until rpm starts to decrease again, normally one turn to reach peak rpm again then two turns thereafter to provide the required margin from peak. Always ensure mixture changes are carried out slowly and time is permitted for the change to take effect.

The exhaust gas temperature (EGT) indicator may be used as an aid for mixture leaning in cruise flight at 75% power or less. Lean the mixture to establish the peak EGT, and then enrich the mixture till approximately 50ºF rich of peak EGT. Peak EGT will correspond to the peak rpm described above, however it is easier to see the peak, since the change in temperature is larger, and there is less chance of power loss from leaning too far. There is normally a small reference needle on the EGT gauge, which is manually set to the peak on leaning, for monitoring of changes.

Cessna specifies leaning for takeoff at altitudes above 3000ft, however they provide very little guidance on how to do this.

Leaning for a normal take-off may be carried out during the engine run-up at 1700rpm in the same way as described above. This setting is normally maintained to top of climb although further leaning during extended climbs of more than 3000ft may be needed. At 1700rpm the EGT is too cool to obtain accurate information, however it may be checked against the reference line during the climb, if the reference line is known to have been set in similar conditions.

If maximum power is required, the mixture must be leaned at full power.

Where not specified, 3000ft must be taken to be a density altitude, since significant reduction of performance will be experienced at high outside temperatures at 3000ft pressure altitude if no leaning is carried out.

During low power operations on the ground, it is best to err towards the lean side, since at low operating temperatures there is a higher risk of spark plug fouling and other negative effects of carbon build up on the engine from the mixture being set too rich, than there is of detonation or overheating from the mixture being too lean.

Engine Gauges

Any change in altitude or throttle position will require a readjusting of the mixture setting.

Engine operation is monitored by the following instruments:
- ✈ Tachometer;
- ✈ Oil pressure gauge;
- ✈ Oil temperature gauge;
- ✈ Exhaust Gas Temperature (EGT) gauge (1979 on);
- ✈ Cylinder Head Temperature (CHT) gauge (optional).

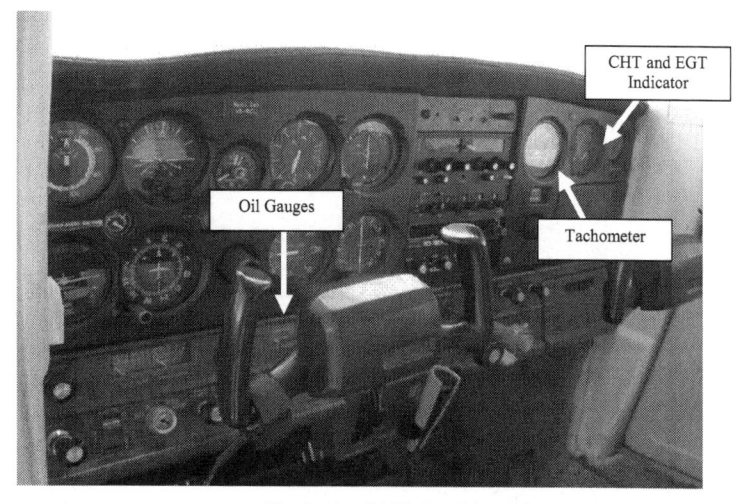

Illustration 5d Engine Gauges

Tachometer

The engine-driven mechanical tachometer is located near the upper center portion of the instrument panel. The instrument is calibrated in increments of 100 rpm and indicates engine and propeller speed. An hours meter inside the tachometer dial records elapsed engine time and runs at full speed only when the engine develops full power. Hence total flight time from chock to chock is usually higher than 'tacho. time'.

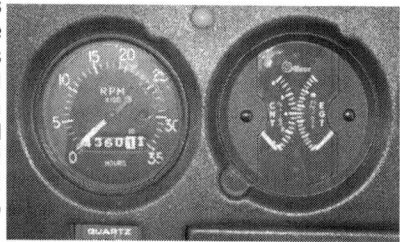

Illustration 5e Tachometer and Modified Post-manufacture CHT/EGT Gauge

Pressure and Temperature Gauges
The oil pressure and temperature gauges are located on the left bottom side of the instrument panel. The normal operating range on both gauges is marked by a green arc.

Illustration 5f Engine Oil Temperature and Pressure Gauges

The temperature gauge is an electric resistance type device powered by the electrical system. The pressure gauge is a mechanical direct reading device based on a "bordon tube" design.

Indications vary from engine to engine, however any deviation from the green range requires immediate action. This may include reduction in power, increasing airspeed, richening mixture as applicable and contemplation of a landing when possible.

CHT Gauge
The Cylinder Head Temperature (CHT) indicator, if installed, is a more accurate means of measuring the engine operating condition. The CHT is not part of the standard engine instruments provided by the manufacturer, but, because of it's usefulness, it may be fitted as a post manufacturer modification.
The CHT is a direct indication of engine temperature compared with oil temperature which is surrounding the engine and has inertia and damping effects.

As this is one of the hottest part of the engine probes are often prone to failure, and may fail in a high or low position. Indications must be interpreted in conjunction with the oil temperature and pressure readings to ensure integrity of the signal and a full picture of the engine operating condition.

EGT Indicator
The Exhaust Gas Temperature (EGT) indicator is normally located near the tachometer and installed standard on aircraft after 1978. A thermocouple probe in the muffler tailpipe measures exhaust gas temperature and transmits it to the indicator. Exhaust gas temperature varies with fuel-to-air ratio, power, and rpm. The indicator is equipped with a manually positioned reference pointer.

Induction System and Carb. Heat
The engine receives air through an intake in the lower portion of the engine cowling. The intake is covered by an air filter which removes dust and other foreign matter from the induction air. Airflow passing through the filter enters the inlet in the up-draught-type carburettor underneath the engine intake.

Illustration 5g Air Filter

The air then is mixed with the fuel and ducted to the engine cylinders through intake manifold tubes.
In the event carburettor ice is encountered or the intake filter becomes blocked, alternate heated air can be used. A selector knob mounted on the instrument panel (see picture above) controls the selection of hot air to the induction system. The control operates a Bowden cable which terminates at a butterfly valve in the carburettor air mixing box.

Air enters this box from two sources:
- Normal cold induction air – through the intake mounted in the nose and protected by a filter screen;
- Hot air intake, mounted on the starboard front shelf of the engine cowling connected to a heat exchanger unit fitted to the engine exhaust system.

The purpose of the hot air is to prevent the formation of ice in the induction line of the engine. Ice formation of this type is recognized by a gradual or sharp drop in the engine rpm and/or rough running. When icing is suspected, the hot air knob (Carb. Heat) should be pulled into the fully out position. Confirmation of the icing will be by a further drop (from the hot air), followed by an increase when the ice is cleared.

Operation of the carb heat should be always fully out or in, partial operation may increase icing due to small heat raising temperature to the icing range. A functioning test for the system should be carried out at 1700 rpm during engine run up. With the selection of hot air, a positive drop in power should occur. Use of full carburettor heat at full throttle during flight will result in a loss of approximately 150 rpm.

It should be remembered that heated air is obtained from an **unfiltered** outside source. For this reason, Carb.Heat should never be used on the ground for prolonged time, and never in areas where there is a risk of ingestion of foreign matter. Dust, grass seeds, and other ground based debris inducted into the intake system of the engine is a major contributing factor to early engine wear and a common cause of engine failures after take-off. When operating under high dust conditions, the carburettor heat system should not be used unless carburettor ice is suspected and the induction air filter should be serviced after the flight.

Engine Lubrication

A wet sump, pressure lubricated oil system is employed. Oil is supplied from a sump on the bottom of the engine. A wet sump engine has a sump attached to it in which the oil is stored. The capacity of the sump is 6 imperial quarts of which 2 quarts are unusable. Oil is drawn from the sump through the engine-driven oil pump to a thermostatically controlled bypass valve. If the oil is cold, the bypass valve allows the oil to bypass the oil cooler and flow directly to the oil filter. If the oil is hot, the oil is routed to the engine oil cooler mounted on the left forward side of the engine and then to the filter. The filtered oil then enters a pressure relief valve which regulates engine oil pressure by allowing excessive oil to return to the sump, while the balance of the pressure oil is circulated to the various engine parts for engine lubrication and cooling, Oil is returned by gravity to the engine sump.

Because oil viscosity changes with temperature and due to the nature of this system, there will be a small change in the pressure with changes in operating temperatures, the warmer the temperature the lower the pressure. It should be noted that any large increases in temperature or decreases in pressure, or deviation from normal operating (green) range are an indication of possible malfunction. Discontinuation of the flight or landing at the nearest suitable location should be contemplated.

Oil should be added if the level is below 4 quarts. The oil tank dipstick is fastened to the oil filler cap. To minimize loss of oil through the breather, fill to 5 quarts for normal flights of less than three hours. Access to the filler cap is through the inspection panel on the right side of the engine. Make sure that the filler cap is firmly on. Over turning may result in damage to the cap or difficulty in loosening, under turning may result in loss of oil or cap during flight.

Illustration 5h Oil Dipstick

=Oil temperature and pressure gauges are fitted on the lower part of the instrument panel. If normal oil pressure is not indicated within 30 seconds of starting, the engine should be shut down immediately.

Ignition System

The necessary high-tension electrical current for the spark plugs comes from self-contained spark generation and distribution units called the magnetos. The magneto consists of a magnet that is rotated near a conductor which has a coil of wire around it. The rotation of the magnet induces an electrical current to flow in the coil. The voltage is fed to each spark plug at the appropriate time, causing a spark to jump between the two electrodes. This spark ignites the fuel/air mixture.

While the engine is running, the magneto is a completely self-sufficient source of electrical energy, and does not require electrical power from the battery or alternator.

The aircraft is equipped with a dual ignition system, that is, two engine-driven magnetos, each controlling one of the two spark plugs in each cylinder. A dual ignition system is safer, providing backup in event of failure of one ignition system, and results in more even and efficient fuel combustion. The dual system has

Illustration 5i Magneto

an added bonus of being able to isolate left and right parts for easy plug and magneto fault finding during engine run up.

The left magneto is fitted on the left hand side of the engine, as viewed from the pilot's seat, and the right magneto to the right side, although the selector switch is normally fitted in reverse, (see Ignition Switch below).
On the 1978 models, the left magneto fires the plugs fitted into the bottom of the cylinders, and the right magneto fires the top plugs. On all later models, the left magneto fires the left bottom and right top plugs, and the right magneto fires the right bottom and left top plugs, providing better redundancy, since the bottom plugs are more prone to fouling.

Ignition Switch

Ignition and starter operation is controlled by a rotary type switch located on the left bottom side of the instrument panel. The switch is labeled clockwise: OFF, R, L, BOTH and START. When the ignition switch is placed on L (left) the left ignition circuit is working and the right ignition circuit is off and vice versa. The engine should be operated on both magnetos (BOTH position) in all situations apart from magneto checks and in an emergency. When the switch is rotated to the spring-loaded START position (with master switch in the ON position), the starter is energized and the starter will crank the engine. When the switch is released, it will automatically return to the BOTH position.

Dead Cut and Live Mag. Check

It is important to realise if the ignition is live, the engine may be started by moving the propeller, even though the master switch is OFF. The magneto does not require outside source of electrical energy.

Placing the ignition switch to OFF position grounds the primary winding of the magneto system so that it no longer supplies electrical power. With a loose or broken wire, or some other fault, switching the ignition to OFF may not ground both magnetos.
To prevent this situation, just before shutting an engine down, a "dead-cut" of the ignition system should be made.

The dead-cut check is made by switching the ignition momentarily to OFF and a sudden loss of power should be apparent. This is carried out most effectively from R, not from Both, to prevent inadvertent sticking in OFF.

On start up, a live mag check is performed, to ensure both magnetos are working before taxi. This is not a system function check detailed below, as the engine is still cold and plugs may be fouled, rather just a check to ensure both magnetos are working by switching from Both to L, then R, and back to Both, noting a small drop from Both in L and R positions. A dead-cut check may be carried out at the same time.

The engine will run on just one magneto, but the burning is less efficient, not as smooth as on two, and there is a slight drop in rpm.
The magneto check to confirm both magnetos and plugs are operational should be made at 1700 rpm as follows:
- Move ignition switch to R position and note the rpm;
- Then move switch back to BOTH to clear the other set of plugs;
- Move switch to the L position, note the rpm and return to BOTH position.

Rpm drop should not exceed 125 rpm on either magneto or show greater than 50 rpm difference between magnetos.

An absence of rpm drop may be an indication of faulty grounding of one side of the ignition system, a disconnected ground lead at the magneto, or possibly the magneto timing is set too far in advance.
Excessive drop or differential normally indicates a faulty magneto.

Fouled spark plugs (lead deposits on the spark plug preventing ignition) are indicated by rough running usually combined with a large drop in rpm (i.e. one or more cylinders not firing). This is due to one of the two plugs becoming fouled, normally the lower plug. Plug fouling, if not excessive, may be burnt off.
Run the engine at a correct or slightly lean mixture setting and a high power setting (+/-2000rpm) for a few minutes, caution engine temperatures and surrounds.

Engine Cooling

The engine cooling system is designed to keep the engine temperature within those limits designed by the manufacturer. Engine temperatures are kept within acceptable limits by:
- The oil that circulates within the engine;
- The air cooling system that circulates fresh air around the engine compartment.

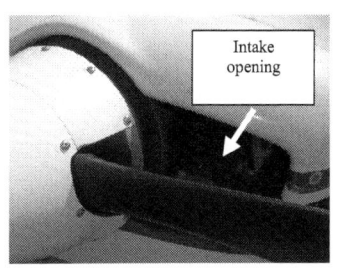

Illustration 5j Air Intake

The engine is air-cooled by exposing the cylinders and their cooling fins to the airflow. Air for engine cooling enters through two openings in the front of the engine cowling. The cooling air is directed around the cylinders and other areas of the engine by baffling, and is then exhausted through an opening at the bottom aft edge of the cowling. No manual cooling system control is provided.

Air cooling is least effective at high power and low airspeed, for instance on take-off and climb. At high airspeed and low power, for instance on descent, the cooling might be too effective. It is therefore important to monitor the cylinder-head temperature gauge throughout the flight, and also on the ground when air-cooling will be poor.

If excessive temperatures are noted in flight, the cooling of the engine can be improved by:
- Making the mixture richer (extra fuel has a cooling effect in the cylinders, because more fuel is evaporated, so rich mixture cools better that a lean mixture);
- Reducing the engine power;
- Increasing the airspeed;

The propeller spinner in addition to streamlining and balance is a director for the cooling air, and so the aeroplane should generally not be operated without the spinner.

Fuel System

Fuel is supplied to the engine from two integral wing tanks. From these, fuel flows by gravity feed through the fuel shut-off valve and the fuel strainer, manual primer to the carburettor.

The fuel capacity is:
- ✈ Standard Tanks - Total usable fuel 24.5 US gallons (91 litres), total capacity 26 US gallons (98 litres);
- ✈ Long Range Tanks - Total usable fuel 37.5 US gallons (141 litres), total capacity 39 US gallon (147 litres).

The long range tanks, although specified in the pilot's operating handbook, are a relatively uncommon installation, and not specified on the type certification data. Some Cessna 152's with standard tanks may have post manufacturer auxiliary tanks installed to increase fuel capacity.

The amount of fuel we can put into fuel tanks is limited by the volume of the tanks, and therefore usable fuel is always provided in volume, such as gallons and litres. However, the carburettor and engine are only sensitive to the mass of fuel, and not to the volume. The engine will consume a certain mass (lbs or kgs) of fuel per hour. Fuel has a wide variation in specific gravity (weight of fuel per volume) mostly depending on temperature and type of fuel. Therefore, variations in specific gravity of fuel can have a significant effect on the mass of fuel in the tanks and therefore the range and endurance.
For practical purposes the specific gravity of Avgas is taken as 0.72 kgs/lt.

The fuel valve is located on the floor of the cockpit between the pilot and co-pilot seats. The valve has two positions: ON and OFF.
With the valve in the ON position, fuel flows through a strainer to the carburettor. The fuel strainer is mounted at the firewall in the lower engine compartment. The strainer is equipped with a quick-drain valve which provides a means of draining trapped water and sediment from the fuel system. The quick-drain control is located

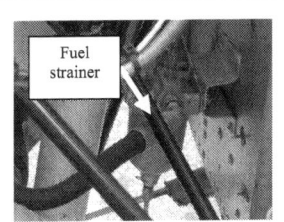

Illustration 6a Fuel Strainer

adjacent to the oil dipstick and is accessible through the oil dipstick door.
The strainer should be opened for a few seconds before the first flight of the day to ensure removal of any water and sediment, preferably into a sample cup for analysis.

A balance tube connects the two tanks and aims to ensure even pressure and thus even feeding from both tanks. Each tank contains it's own fuel line which is routed down the side of the fuselage to the fuel shut off valve on the cockpit floor.

Fuel Measuring and Indication

Fuel quantity is measured by two float-type fuel quantity transmitters (one in each tank), and indicated by two electrically-operated fuel quantity indicators on the lower left portion of the instrument panel.

The full position of float produces a minimum resistance through transmitter, permitting maximum current flow through the fuel quantity indicator and maximum pointer deflection.

As fuel level is lowered, resistance in the transmitter is increased, producing a decreased current flow through the fuel quantity indicator and a smaller pointer deflection. An empty tank is indicated by a red line and letter E. When an indicator shows an empty tank, approximately 0.75 gallons remain in the tank as unusable fuel.

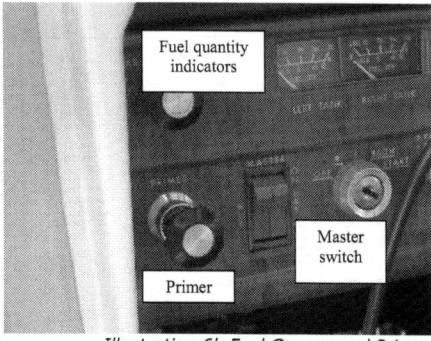

Illustration 6b Fuel Gauges and Primer

The float gauge will indicate variations with changes in the position of fuel in the tanks and cannot be relied upon for accurate reading during skids, slips, or unusual attitudes.

Considering the nature of the system, takeoff is not recommended with less than 1 hour total fuel remaining. Fuel quantity should always be confirmed by dipstick during the preflight inspection and on intermediate stops enroute.

Priming

Priming is carried out by use of a manual pump located on left bottom corner of the instrument panel, which is connected by fuel lines to all the engine cylinders.
Operation of the pump plunger forces fuel directly into the engine cylinders bypassing the carburettor.
Although priming may be achieved by operation of the throttle with an accelerator pump (as described below), the primer is a more effective method and is the method specified in the pilots operating handbook.

Priming the engine is normally required when starting a cold engine, when the fuel in the carburettor is reluctant to vaporize. One to three pumps of the primer is recommended depending on the temperature and should be carried out immediately prior to starting.

by D. Bruckert & O. Roud © 2004

If priming is carried out too early the fuel is ineffective in the start cycle, but effective in washing oil from the cylinder walls and causing additional frictional wear on start.

The primer should be locked when the engine is running to avoid excessive fuel being drawn through the priming line into the cylinders, which could cause an engine failure from the fuel/air mixture becoming too rich.

Accelerator Pump

From 1980 an accelerator pump was incorporated in the carburettor. The accelerator pump is a small piston, activated by the throttle control linkage, that forces additional fuel into the carburettor throat when the throttle is opened.

The primary purpose of an accelerator pump is to assist in 'accelerating' the fuel input to the engine when the throttle is opened rapidly.
Without an accelerator pump, when the throttle is opened quickly, there is a chance of the engine mis-firing or stalling from a too lean mixture, since air has less weight and thus less inertia than fuel and moves quicker.

Hesitation, mis-fire or momentary engine stall on opening of the throttle may be a sign of accelerator pump wear.

A secondary function of the accelerator pump is to permit use of the throttle for priming, however as noted above, the preferred technique is to use the primer pump, since this provides fuel more directly to the cylinders than the accelerator pump.

Fuel Venting

Fuel system venting is essential to system operation and is necessary to allow normal fuel flow or pressure venting as fuel is used. Blockage of the venting system will result in a decreasing fuel flow and eventual engine stoppage.

A vent line is installed in the outboard end of the left fuel cell and extends overboard down through the lower wing skin (as illustrated opposite). The inboard end of the vent line extends into the fuel tank, then forward and slightly upward. A vent valve is installed on the inboard end of the vent line inside the fuel tank, and a crossover vent line connects the two tanks for positive ventilation. The right fuel tank filler cap is also vented, and some on early 1978 models both caps are vented.

Illustration 6c Fuel Tank Vent

The vent line opens to the highest part of the tank, therefore it is normal if the tanks are full to see a small amount of overflow fuel leaking through the fuel vent.

During flight, the left wing tank is pressure vented, facing into the relative air flow, while the wing cap vent is in an area of low pressure. Despite the intended effect of the balance tube between the tanks, this sometimes results in a tendency for fuel to feed from the left wing at a higher rate than the right wing. As there is only one fuel selector position, nothing can be done if uneven feeding occurs, however maintaining balanced flight whenever possible will help. If uneven feeding becomes severe the situation should be checked by a maintenance organisation, as there is possibly a blockage in the fuel lines or balance tube.

Fuel Drains

The fuel system is equipped with drain valves to provide a means for the examination of fuel in the system for contamination and grade. The system should be examined before the first flight of every day and after each refuelling, by using the sampler cup to drain fuel from the wing tanks and sump.

Fuel drains are spring-loaded valves at the bottom of each fuel tank. There is usually a drop in air temperature overnight and, if the tank is not full, the fuel tanks' walls will become cold and there will be a lot more condensation than if the tanks were full of fuel. The water, as it is heavier than fuel, will accumulate at the bottom of the fuel tanks.

If water is found in the tank, fuel should be drained until all the water has been removed, and wings should be rocked to allow any other water to gravitate to the fuel strainer drain valve.

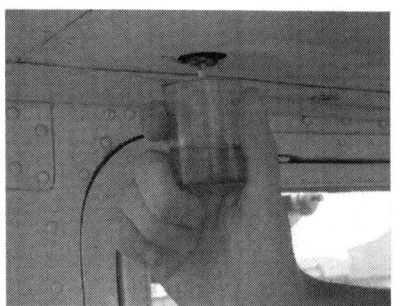

Illustration 6d Fuel Tank Under-wing Drain

The Cessna 152 does not have bladder tanks fitted, so any small rubber particles in the fuel are normally a sign that the rubber o-ring which seals the fuel drain is perishing. This can be accompanied by fuel staining around the fuel drain. Advice from your maintenance organisation should be sought since this can lead to a major fuel leak.

On the following page a schematic of the fuel system is shown.

Fuel System Schematic

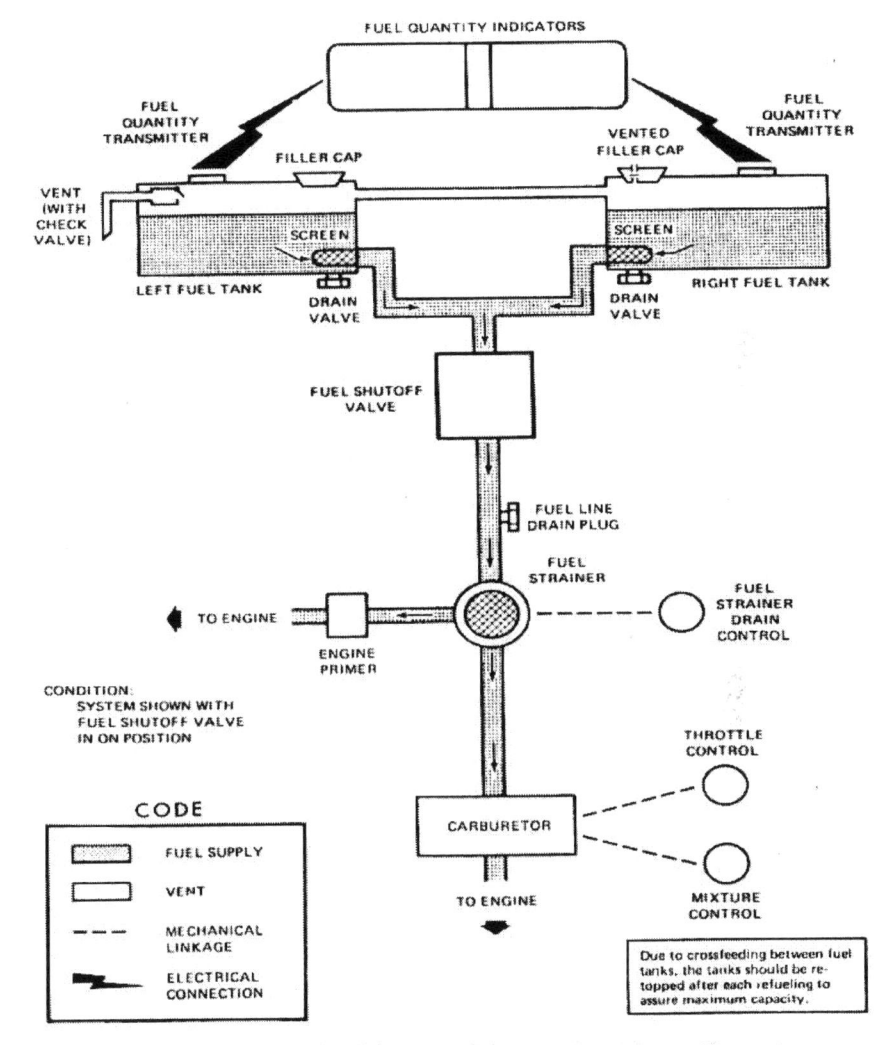

Fuel System (Standard and Long Range)

Illustration 6e Fuel System Schematic

Electrical System

Electrical energy for the aircraft is supplied by a 28-volt, direct-current, single wire, negative ground, electrical system.

Battery

A 24-volt battery supplies power for starting and furnishes a reserve source of power in the event of alternator failure.

The battery capacity will be either
- ✦ 14 amp-hour standard (early 1978);
- ✦ 17 amp-hour optional (early 1978);
- ✦ 12.75 amp-hour standard;
- ✦ 15.5 amp-hour optional.

Figure 7a Battery Installation Post 1980

The amp-hour is the capacity of the battery to provide a current for a certain time. A 14 amp-hour battery is capable of steadily supplying a current of 1 amp for 14 hours and 7 amp for 2 hours and so on.

The battery is mounted on the right forward side of the firewall, as indicated in the picture above. Pre 1980 models additionally have a battery box for mounting.

Batteries should not be serviced unless under supervision of an approved maintenance organisation. Although most batteries are refilled with distilled water, some require refilling with electrolyte comprising a mix of water and acid, the composition of which is important to proper battery operation. Servicing requirements specific to the battery part number are contained within the maintenance manuals and service bulletins kept by the maintenance provider.

Alternator

A 60 amp engine-driven alternator is the normal source of power during flight and maintains a battery charge, controlled by a voltage regulator/alternator control unit.

A 28-volt electrical system with 24-volt battery means that because the alternator provides 28-volt power, which is more than battery power, the battery charge is maintained while in normal operations.

An alternator needs a small pre-charge, approximately 3 Volts to operate. In the case of a battery which is completely discharged (flat), if the engine is started by hand swinging the propeller, the alternator will not be capable of generating a charge. It is far preferable to find a ground power source, even for example a truck battery, and follow the external power starting procedure (see further below).

Ground (External) Power Receptacle

An optional ground power receptacle may be installed for easy connection of an external electrical supply. The ground power receptacle is mounted on the left side of the firewall with access via a small door in the engine cowling.

Ground power, or external supply of electrical power, can be very useful for extended use of electrical equipment on the ground, for operation of pre-heat in extreme cold weather operations, and for starting when the battery is flat.

Before connecting an external power source, it is important that the master switch be turned "ON". This will close the battery contactor and enable the battery to absorb transient voltages which otherwise might damage the electronic equipment. It will also provide excitation of the alternator field in the event that the battery is completely dead. Because the procedure is not very familiar, there may be a tendency to forget this important step, readers are reminded, for this reason unfamiliar procedures should always be conducted with reference to the Pilot's Operating Handbook.

Electrical Equipment

The following standard equipment on the Cessna 152 requires electrical power for operation (there may be additional optional equipment which uses electrical power):

- Fuel quantity indicators;
- Engine temperature gauges;
- Turn Coordinator;
- All internal and external lights, including warning lights;
- Pitot heat;
- Wing flaps;
- Starter;
- All avionics equipment.

System Protection and Distribution

Electrical power for electrical equipment and electronic installations is supplied through the split bus bar. The bus bar is interconnected by a wire and attached to the circuit breakers on the lower, centre of the instrument panel.

The circuit breakers are provided to protect electrical equipment from current overload. If there is an electrical overload or short-circuit, a circuit breaker (CB) will pop out and break the circuit so that no current can flow through it. It is normal procedure (provided there is no smell or other sign of burning or overheating) to reset a CB once only, after a cooling period, by pushing

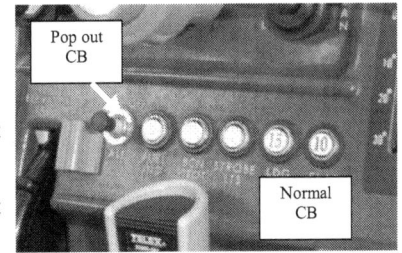

Figure 7b Circuit Breakers

it back in. If the circuit breaker pops again, the flight should be continued, without use of the faulty equipment, plan a diversion if necessary to the nearest suitable airport.

Most of the electrical circuits in the aeroplane are protected by "push-to-reset" type circuit breakers. However, alternator output and some others are protected by a "pull-off" type circuit breaker to allow for voluntary isolation in case of a malfunction.
Electrical circuits which are not protected by circuit breakers are the battery contactor closing (external power) circuit, clock circuit, and flight hour recorder circuit.
These circuits are protected by fuses mounted adjacent to the battery and are sometimes termed "hot wired or hot bus" connections.

The master switch controls the operation of the battery and alternation system.
The switch is an interlocking split rocker type with the battery mode on the right hand side and the alternator mode on the left hand side. This arrangement allows the battery to be on line without the alternator, however, operation of the alternator without the battery on the line is not possible.
The switch is labeled BAT and ALT and is located on the left-hand side of the instrument panel.
Continued operation with the alternator switch OFF will reduce battery power low enough to open the battery contactor, remove power from the alternator field, and prevent the alternator restart. This is important to remember if you are starting an aeroplane by other means because of a flat battery.

The ammeter, located on the upper right side of the instrument panel, indicates the flow of current, in amperes, from the alternator to the battery or from the battery to the aircraft electrical system.
When the engine is operating and the master switch is ON, the ammeter indicates the charging rate applied to the battery.

When the ammeter needle is deflected right of center, the current flows into the battery and indicates the battery charge rate.
When the ammeter needle is deflected left of center, the current flows from the battery the battery and the battery is therefore discharging.

With battery switch ON and no alternator output, the ammeter will indicate a discharge from the battery, because the battery is providing current for the electrical circuits that are switched on.

If the alternator is ON, but incapable of supplying sufficient power to the electrical circuits, the battery must make up the balance and there will be some flow of current from the battery. The ammeter will

Illustration 7c Ammeter

show a discharge. In this case, the load on the electrical system should be reduced by switching off unnecessary electrical equipment until the ammeter indicates a charge.
Indication of charge from the system to the battery more than temporarily may indicate more serious problems and should be checked out immediately.

The aircraft is equipped with an automatic over-voltage protection system consisting of an over-voltage sensor, incorporated behind the instrument panel for 1978 models, and in the alternator control unit for 1979 and later models, and a red warning light near the ammeter. The switch is labelled 'HIGH VOLTAGE' on 1978 models, and 'LOW VOLTAGE' in 1979 and later models.

In both cases, in the event an over-voltage condition occurs, the over-voltage sensor automatically removes the alternator field current and shuts down the alternator, and the red warning light will then turn on, indicating to the pilot that the battery is supplying all electrical power and can be checked on the ammeter. In both cases, the warning light will also turn on any time the alternator is removed from the system, and can be tested by momentarily selecting the the alternator off (turning off the ALT portion of the master switch). Note: In an operational respect, it may be useful to think of the difference being that initially the switch was labelled for the cause, and later for the effect.

If the over voltage condition that caused the trip-off was transient, the sensor may be reset by turning the both sides of the master switch OFF and back ON again.
If the light illuminates again, a power supply malfunction has occurred, the alternator should not be reset again. The flight should be terminated as soon as practical, bearing in mind the consequences of an electrical supply from battery source only, as detailed in the POH.

Illumination of the low-voltage light may occur during low rpm conditions with an electrical load on the system, such as during the taxi at low rpm. Under these conditions, the light will go out at higher rpm, and the master switch need not be recycled since an over-voltage condition has not occurred to de-activate the alternator.

It is possible for the over-voltage sensor to malfunction, resulting over voltage condition without activation of the alternator trip-off and warning light, or for the warning light to illuminate without an alternator trip-off. Both situations illustrate the importance of monitoring the ammeter reading along with other instruments as part of normal airmanship. In the case of an over-voltage, the alternator will need to be removed quickly from the system to prevent further damage to electrical equipment, this procedure is outlined in the Pilot's Operating Handbook. In the case of a light illuminating without a discharge indication on the alternator, the indicator only is defective, and providing this can be confirmed, the flight may be continued to land at a point of maintenance. This situation is considerably less dangerous, and as such is only detailed in the Cessna maintenance manuals.

On the following page a schematic of the electrical system can be seen.

… CESSNA 152 TRAINING MANUAL

Electrical System Schematic

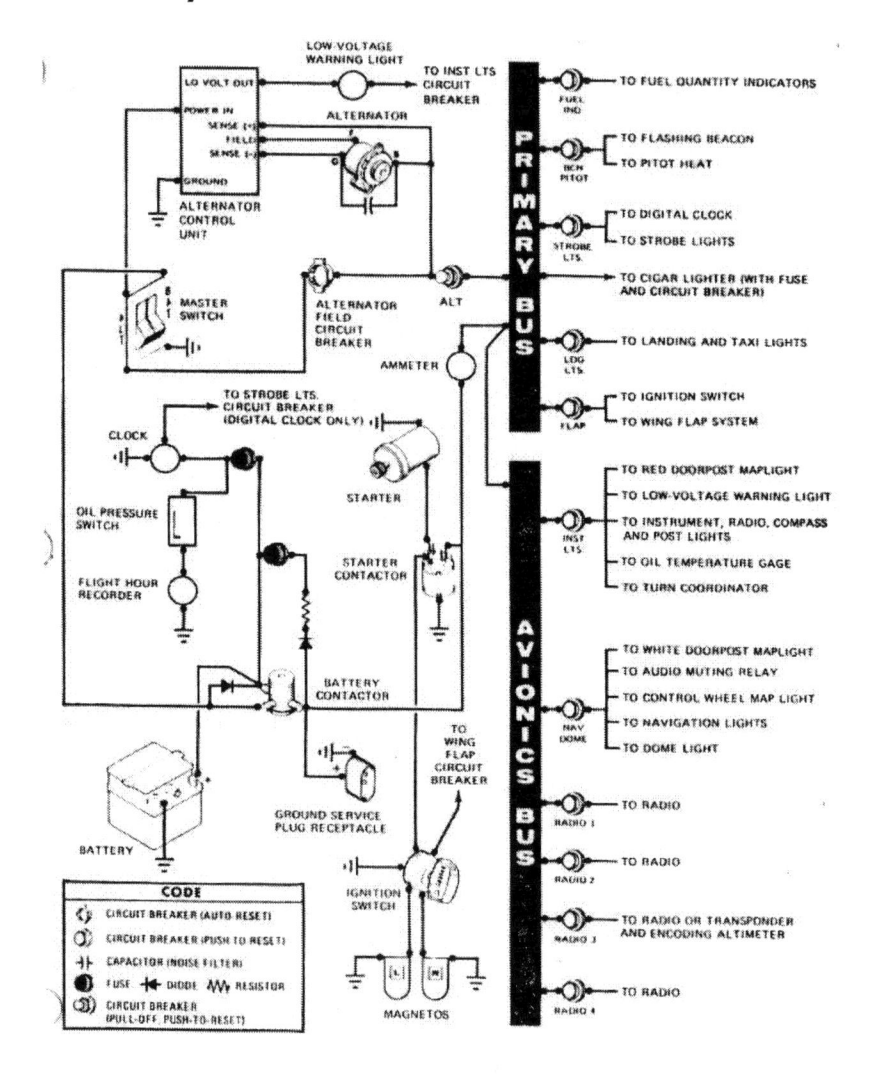

Electrical System

Illustration 7d Electrical System Schematic

Flight Instruments and Associated Systems

The aircraft is equipped with the following standard flight instruments:
- **Attitude Indicator:** or artificial horizon, a gyro which operates on vacuum pressure and provides a visual indication of flight attitude. A knob at the bottom of the instrument is provided for adjustment of the miniature aeroplane to the horizon bar on the case;
- **Directional Indicator:** a gyro which operates on vacuum pressure, and displays aeroplane heading on a compass card. A knob on the lower left edge of the instrument is used to adjust the compass card to the magnetic compass to correct for any precession;
- **Airspeed Indicator:** operates with dynamic and static pressure and is calibrated in knots. The instrument has limitation markings in form of white, green and yellow arcs and a red line;
- **Altimeter:** operates on static pressure and displays aeroplane altitude in feet. A knob near the lower left edge of the instrument provides adjustment of the barometric scale to the required setting – (for example QNH, QNE, or QFE);
- **Vertical Speed Indicator** operates on static pressure and displays aeroplane rate of climb or descent in feet per minute;
- **Turn and Slip Indicator** a gyro which operates electric power (providing redundancy for the attitude indicator), for the rate of turn indication, and a gravity ball for slip indication.

Vacuum System

Suction is necessary to operate the main gyro instruments, consisting of the attitude indicator and directional indicator. Suction is provided by a dry-type, engine-driven, vacuum pump. A suction relief valve, to control system pressure, is connected between the pump inlet and the instruments. A suction gauge is fitted on the instrument panel and indicates suction at the gyros. A suction range of 3 to 5 inches of mercury below atmospheric pressure is acceptable. The normal range at cruise rpm is between 4.6 and 5.4 inches.

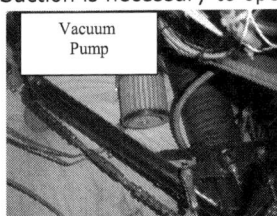

Illustration 8a Vacuum Pump

If the vacuum pressure is too low, the airflow will be reduced, the gyro's rotor will not run at the required speed, and the gyro instruments will be unreliable. Low vacuum pressure can have a serious effect on instrument flying, since the attitude and direction gyros' unreliability is sometimes not picked up until the aircraft is off course or in an unusual attitude. Beginning with 1983 models, a low vacuum warning light was fitted which illuminates when the vacuum pressure drops below 3 inches.
If the vacuum pressure is too high, the gyro rotors speed will be too fast and the gyro may be damaged.

A schematic of the system is shown on the following page.

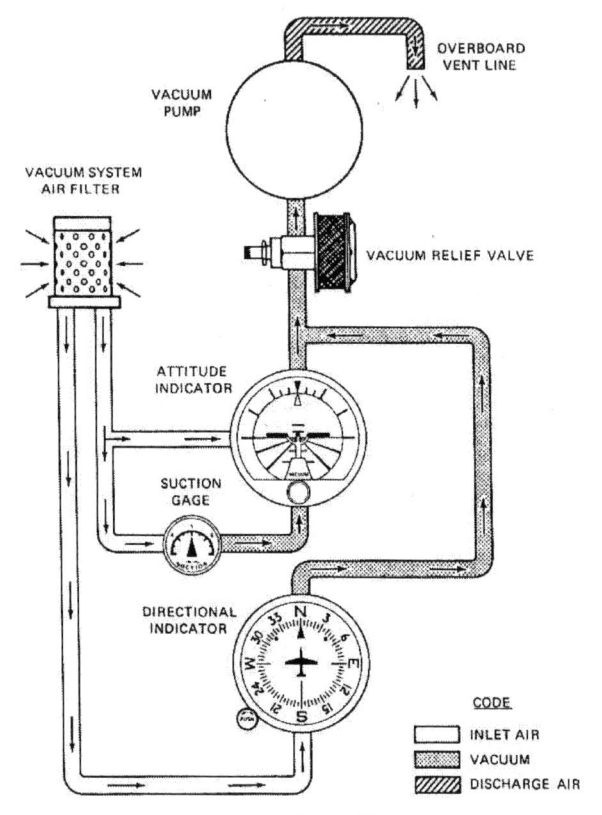

Vacuum System Schematic

Illustration 8b Vacuum System Schematic

Pitot-Static System

The pitot-static system supplies dynamic air pressure to the airspeed indicator and static air pressure to the airspeed indicator, vertical speed indicator and altimeter.
The system is composed of a pitot tube mounted on the lower surface of the left wing, an external static port on the lower left side of the forward fuselage, and associated plumbing necessary to connect the instrument to the sources.

The heated pitot system consists of a heating element in the pitot tube, and a switch labeled PITOT HT on the lower left side of the instrument panel.
When the pitot heat switch is turned ON, the element in the pitot tube is heated electrically to avoid ice building on the pitot tube in possible icing conditions.

The pitot tube and static vent should not be damaged or obstructed, otherwise false reading from the relevant flight instruments could degrade the safety of the flight. They should be carefully checked in the preflight inspection.
The pitot cover is used to prevent water or insects accumulating in the tube during parking. The pitot tube and static vent should not be tested by blowing in them, since very sensitive instruments are involved.

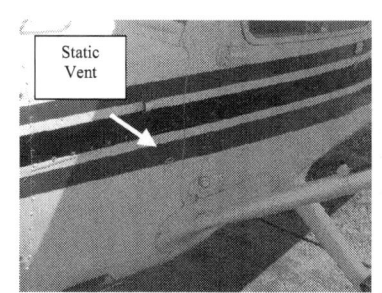

Illustration 8c Static Vent and Pitot Tube

Stall Warning

The aeroplane is equipped with a pneumatic-type stall warning system consisting of an inlet in the leading edge of the left wing, and an air-operated horn near the upper left corner of the windshield.
As the aeroplane approaches a stall, the low pressure of the upper surface of the wings moves forward around the leading edge of the wings. This low pressure creates a differential pressure in the stall warning system which draws air through the warning horn, resulting in an audible warning at approximately 5 to 10 knots above stall in all flight conditions.
The system can be checked during the preflight inspection by covering the vent with a clean cloth and applying suction to the vent opening with your mouth. A sound from the warning horn will confirm that the system is operative.

Accelerometer

An accelerometer is fitted to all aerobat models. The accelerometer contains three needles, one indicates the instantaneous acceleration, and the other two record the maximum and minimum accelerations.

The maximum and minimum acceleration pointers will remain in position until the accelerations are exceeded or the reset is pushed.

Ancillary Systems and Equipment
Lighting

Instrument and control panel lighting is provided by flood lighting, and integral lighting (internally lit equipment) and, optional post lights (individual lights above the instruments).

Two rheostat control knobs on the lower left side of the control panel, labeled PANEL LT and RADIO LT, control intensity of the lighting.
A slide-type switch on the overhead console, labeled PANEL LIGHTS, is used to select flood lighting in the FLOOD position.
Flood lighting consists of a single red flood light in the forward part of the overhead console. To use the flood lighting, rotate the PANEL LT rheostat control knob clockwise to the desired intensity.

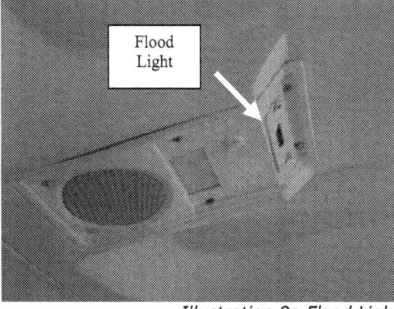

Illustration 9a Flood Light

The external lighting system consists of:
- Navigational lights on the wing tips and top of the rudder;
- Single or optional dual landing/taxi light mounted in the front cowling nose cap or from 1984 on dual landing taxi/light on the left wing leading edge;
- A flashing beacon located on top of the vertical fin;
- Optional strobe lights installed on each wing tip.

All lights are controlled by switches on the lower left side of the instrument panel. The switches are ON in the up position and OFF in the down position.

Cabin Heating and Ventilating System

Heated air and outside air are blended in a cabin manifold just aft of the firewall by adjustment of the heat and air controls.
The temperature and volume of airflow into the cabin is controlled by the push-pull CABIN HT and CABIN AIR control knobs.
The air is vented into the cabin from outlets in the cabin manifold near the pilot's feet. Windshield defrost air is also supplied by a duct leading from the manifold to the outlets below the windshield.
For cabin ventilation, pull the CABIN AIR knob out.
To raise the air temperature, pull the CABIN HT knob partially or fully out as required. Additional direct ventilation may be obtained by opening the adjustable ventilators near the upper left and right corners of the windshield.

The cabin heating system uses warm air from around the engine exhaust. Any leaks in the exhaust system can allow carbon monoxide to enter the cabin.

To minimize the effect of engine fumes, fresh air should always be used in conjunction with cabin heat.

Carbon monoxide is odorless and poisoning will seriously impair human performance, and if not remedied, could be fatal. Personal CO detectors are inexpensive and available at most pilot shops.

Illustration 9b Cabin Air Intake

Avionics Equipment

The minimum standard fitting is a single VHF radio with hand mike and single jack point, however most trainers have a dual place intercom with PTT. Many aircraft have upgrades on the avionics systems so an overview of general operation is included.

Audio Selector

Before operation of any radio installation the audio selector panel should be checked. The audio selector selects the position of the transmitter and receiver for the radio equipment on board.

Illustration 9c Audio Selector

The common selector positions are:

→ Transmitter: Transmit on one, two...

→ Receiver: Listen to Com One/Two or both, Nav instruments
              Listen to each channel on speaker, head phone or select off

Intercom

The intercom sometimes incorporated in the audio select panel contains at least a volume and squelch control. The volume control is for crew volume and squelch for intensity of crew voice activation.

VHF Radio Operations

Once the audio panel has been set, the crew communication established, if required, and the radio switched on, correct operation should be confirmed prior to transmitting. All VHF radio installations will have a squelch selection to check volume and for increased reception when required. This is either in the form of a pull to test button or a rheostat, turned, until activation is heard. Thereafter initial contact should be established if on a manned frequency. Most modern radio installations have an indicator to confirm the transmit button is active. This should be monitored on the first transmission and frequently during initiating radio transmission thereafter.

Transponder

Wherever installed transponders should be switched to standby after start to allow for warm up time. When entering an active runway for departure, until leaving the active runway at the end of the flight, the selector should be in ALT if available or ON.
Many commercial aircraft now contain TCAS and can observe other transponder equipped targets for traffic separation purposes.

The following international transponder codes are useful to remember:

Where no code is specified	2000
Emergencies	7700
Radio failure	7600

NORMAL PROCEDURES

Pre-flight Check

The preflight inspection should be done in anticlockwise direction as indicated in the flight manual, beginning with the interior inspection.

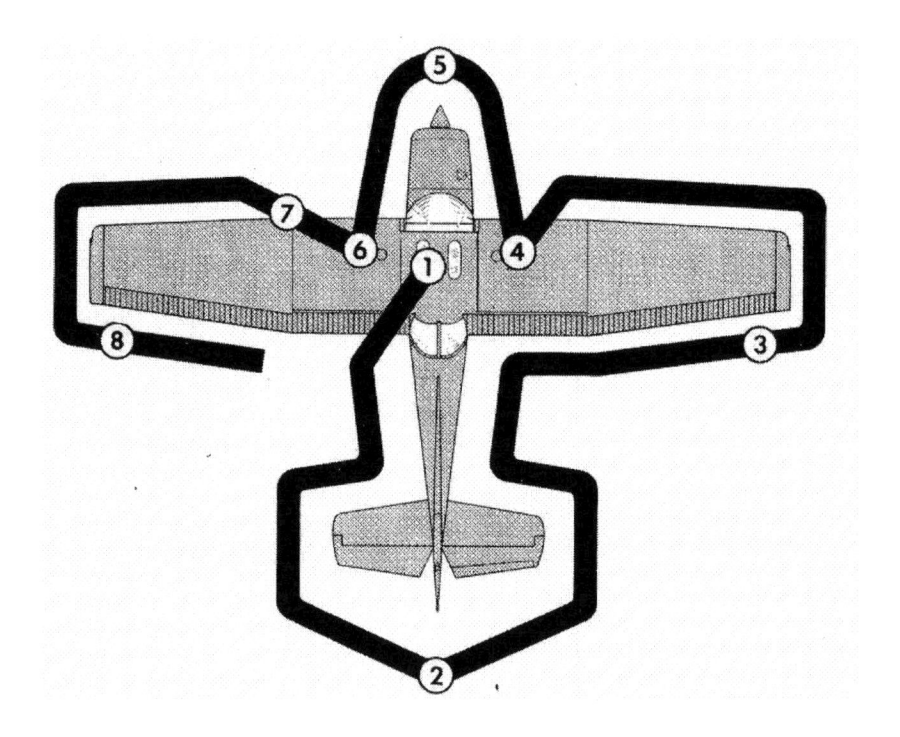

Cabin

Ensure the required documents (certificate of airworthiness, maintenance release, radio license, weight and balance, flight folio, flight manual, and any other flight specific) are on board and valid. Perform a visual inspection of the panel from right to left to ensure all instruments and equipment are in order.

Control lock – REMOVE
Ignition switch – OFF
Lights - OFF except beacon

Master switch – ON
Fuel quantity – CHECK
Flaps level – DOWN
Master switch – OFF
Fuel shutoff valve – ON

Exterior Inspection

Visually check the airplane for general condition during the walk-around inspection, ensuring all surfaces are sound and no signs of structural damage, worked rivets, missing screws, lock wires or loose connections.

Tail Section

Check top, bottom, and side surfaces for any damage, balance weights secure.

Elevator secure and undamaged, linkages and lock wires secure, full and free movement of control surface.

CESSNA 152 TRAINING MANUAL

Linkage and turn-buckles secure, and free movement of control surface.

Beacon, Aerials and rear navigation light undamaged and secure.

Right Wing

Check top, bottom, and side surfaces for any damage. Aerials undamaged and secure.

Ensure flaps do not retract if pushed, flap rollers allow small amount of play in down position.

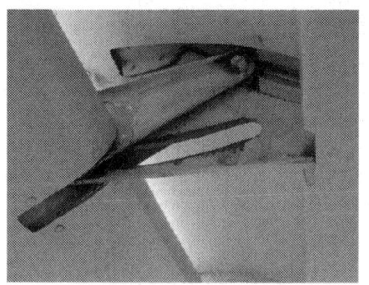

Check for damage to surfaces and flap tracks, freedom of operating linkage and security of all nuts and lockwires.

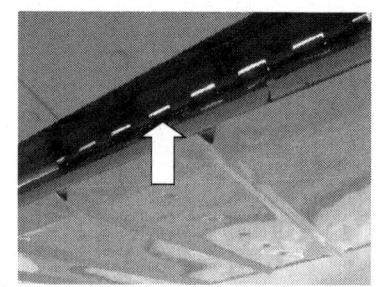

Check for damage to aileron surfaces and security of all hinges, lockwires and flutter weights.

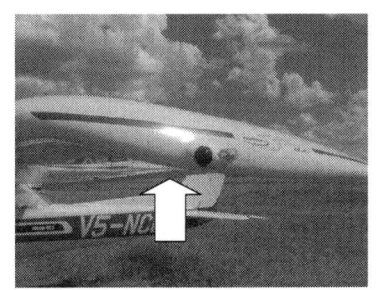

Check condition, security and colour of navigation light.

Check top and bottom wing surfaces for any damage or accumulations on wing. *Ice or excessive dirt must be removed before flight.*

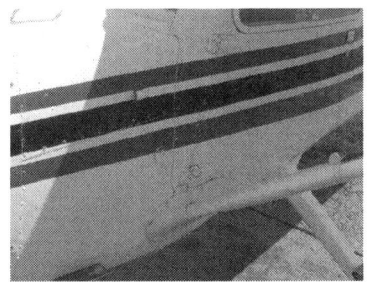

Check condition and security of fairings and wing and wheel struts.

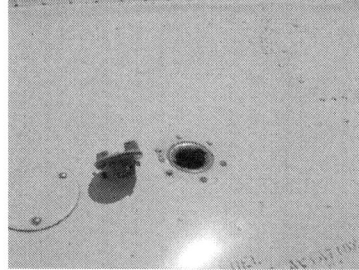

Check visually for desired fuel level using a suitable calibrated dipstick.

Check that fuel cap is secure. (For the type shown the grip should be inline with the longitudinal axis of the aircraft.

🕮 *Never rely on the fuel gauges alone, always check the fuel visually, and thereafter confirm the caps are secure.*

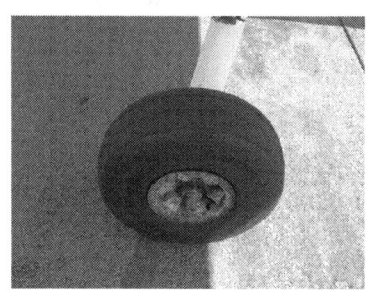

Check tyre for wear, cuts, bruises, and slippage. Recommended tyre pressure should be maintained. Remember, that any drop in temperature of air inside a tyre causes a corresponding drop in air pressure.

CESSNA 152   TRAINING MANUAL

Check for security, condition of hydraulic lines, disc brake and all nuts.

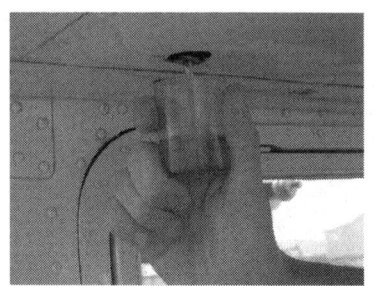

Nose

Confirm security of nuts and split pins, inspect state of tyre.

Check condition and cleanliness of landing light. Air filter should be clear of any dust or other foreign matter. Visually check exhaust for signs of wear, if engine is cool check exhaust is secure.

Use sampler cup and drain a small quantity of fuel from tank sump quick-drain valve to check for water, sediment and proper fuel grade.

Check freedom of operating linkage, and security and state of shimmy damper.

Open inspection cover, check oil level. Minimum oil 4 quarts. Before first flight of the day and after each refuelling, pull out fuel strainer to check the fuel sample. Check strainer drain closed.

Check propeller and spinner for nicks and security. Ensure propeller blades and spinner cover is secure. The propeller may be turned through to assist with pre-start lubrication.

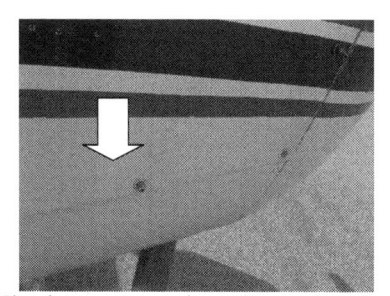

Check security and condition of engine cowling. On the picture nut indicated by arrow is unsecured.

🍂 Always treat the propeller as live.

Differences on the Left Side

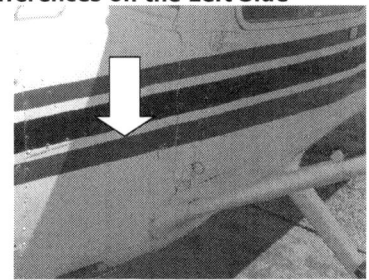

Check the static vent for any sign of blockage.

Remove the pitot tube cover, and check the pitot tube for any sign of blockage.

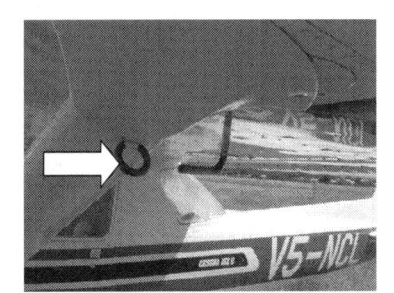

Check the fuel tank vent for security and a clear opening passage.

Final Inspection
Check all chocks and covers are removed and the aircraft is in a position to safely taxi without excessive manoeuvering or power application.

Passenger Brief
After completion of the preflight inspection and preferably before boarding the aircraft, take some time to explain to the passenger the safety equipment, safety harnesses and seat belts, operation of the doors/windows and conduct during flight.

The following items should be included:
- Location and use of the Fire Extinguisher;
- Location and use of the Axe;
- Location of the First Aid Kit;
- Location of emergency and normal water;
- Location of any other emergency or survival equipment;
- Latching, unlatching and fastening of safety harnesses;
- When harnesses should be worn, and when they must be worn;
- Opening, closing and locking of doors and windows;
- Actions in the event of a forced landing or ditching;
- Cockpit safety procedures and passenger conduct during critical phases of flight.

In-Flight Operations

Before Start
Before engine start or priming, all controls should be set in the appropriate positions, the instrument panel set up and pre-start check completed. The panel set up should be a flow through in a logical order (termed a 'flow' pattern) to ensure all equipment is set up correctly, serviceable and accessible, followed by a pre-start check, where applicable.

To provide sufficient fuel for starting the mixture should be full rich at all altitudes. It must be remembered, above approximately 3000ft field elevations the mixture should be leaned after successful starting, to prevent spark plug fouling during low power operations.

Before start checklists may be broken down into 'master off' and 'master on' checks, or more correctly named 'before start', and 'ready to start' checks. The latter items are done only once the aircraft has a start clearance, and is in a position to immediately start the engine. The reason for splitting up the checklist is that certain items such as selecting the master on and priming the engine ideally should not be done too far in advance of the start, as the delay will run down the battery and reduce the effectiveness of the priming.

↣ After completing before start flows, the following before start checklist is recommended:
- **Preflight Inspection** – COMPLETE;
- **Tach/Hobbs/Time** – RECORDED;
- **Passenger Briefing** – COMPLETE;
- **Brakes** – SET/HOLD;
- **Doors** – CLOSED;
- **Seats / Seatbelts** – ADJUSTED, LOCKED;
- **Fuel Selector Valve** – BOTH/CORRECT TANK;
- **Cowl Flaps** – OPEN;
- **Magnetos** – BOTH;
- **Avionics** – OFF;
- **Electrical Equipment** – OFF;
- **Rotating Beacon** – ON.

↣ When ready to start, with the master switch ON and start clearance obtained, prime the engine and complete the remaining 'ready for start' checks:
- **Circuit Breakers** – CHECK IN;
- **Mixture** – RICH / AS REQUIRED*;
- **Prime** – AS REQUIRED (1 to 3 as required);
- **Throttle** – SET approx ½ centimetre*;
- **Propeller Area** – CLEAR.

*With the Lycoming O-235 engine, the mixture should be rich, and the throttle ½cm (¼ inch) open unless a flooded start is required. Other engine types may have different requirements.

Note: Before engaging the propeller, it is vital to check that the propeller area is clear.

Priming

If the engine is cold, it will need to be primed before starting. *Note*, if no heat was felt from the engine area during the preflight, the engine is cold. One to three strokes of the primer will be required depending on the ambient and engine temperature. Even in warm outside temperatures a little priming will improve starting characteristics. Warm engines (i.e. an engine that has been recently running) do not normally require priming.

Priming before start using the throttle should be avoided as the carburettor is located at the bottom of the engine and by advancing the throttle, fuel is primed from carburettor into the engine. As no suction is available from the engine, the fuel may collect in the carburettor. On igniting the engine, this excess fuel may explode in the carburettor and/or begin burning in the intake, damaging the engine. The primer provides fuel directly to the cylinder intake, which reduces the chance of an intake fire.

If over priming occurs, engine clearing, turning the engine over with the mixture at idle cut-off, may be needed. This may be combined with a flooded start procedure. Ensure starter limits, not more than 30 seconds without cooling, are observed.

Start

The engine is started by turning the ignition key into START position, to turn over the engine. The key is spring-loaded back to the BOTH position and can be released once the engine starts.

Before engaging the starter ensure the area ahead and behind is clear. When engaging the starter, always be looking outside, keep one hand on the throttle for adjustment during starting or as the engine fires, and feet on the brakes (light aircraft park brakes are not always self adjusting and may have become weak with brake wear).

Do not crank the engine continuously if the engine fails to start, the starter motor should not be operated continuously for more than 30 seconds. In most cases, if the engine fails to start, one of three things has occurred, either the engine under primed, over primed, or you have omitted an important step, eg placing the fuel selector on. A quick review of the settings, and consideration of the ambient conditions with respect to priming, can prevent further embarrassment, and avoid damage to the battery or starter.

On starting, engine RPM should be kept to a minimum until the engine oil pressure has begun rising. If the throttle has been advanced during starting it is important to ensure it is *immediately* reduced as the engine begins to run. In no circumstances should the engine RPM be allowed to over-rev on start up as the oil will not yet have reached all the moving parts.

Once the engine is started and the oil pressure has stabilised, the throttle should be adjusted to idle at approximately 1000rpm.

After starting, if the oil gauge does not begin to show pressure within 30 seconds, the engine should be shut down immediately and the fault reported to maintenance. Running an engine without oil pressure can cause serious engine damage.

Flooded Start

A flooded start is performed with the mixture at idle cut off, and the throttle fully open. As the engine fires, the mixture is moved towards rich, and the throttle retarded, reasonably simultaneously. This procedure initially feels like it needs three hands, and so generally requires some practice with an instructor before the technique can be performed competently without risk of over-revving the engine.

After Start

After start checks ensure all the critical items are completed prior to taxi. The time spent completing the after takeoff checks properly will also assist with the engine warm-up prior to taxi.

This will include leaning the mixture if the airfield is above 3000ft density altitude, to prevent spark plug fouling during taxi.
A "live mag" check may be done at this point, by selection of the left and right positions to confirm both are live. This confirms both magnetos are operational, it is not an integrity check as the engine is still cold. The purpose of the check is to prevent unnecessary taxiing to the run-up point should one magneto have failed completely.
The direction indicator should be set to the compass for orientation purposes, which is very important at airfields which are not familiar.
The transponder is set to standby or ground for warm up, so that it is ready for use on departure, and any assigned code is confirmed set.
If the flaps were left down during the pre-flight inspection, they should be either retracted, or set for takeoff, to aid visibility and since taxiing with the flaps down signals hijacking.

➢ The following after start checks are recommended:
- **Mixture** – SET for taxi;
- **Magnetos** – CHECKED;
- **Engine Instruments** – CHECKED;
- **Flaps** – RETRACTED/SET FOR TAKEOFF;
- Transponder – STANDBY/GROUND.

Most of the engine warm-up is conducted during taxi. If the engine is cold, for example on first flight of the day, or when it is anticipated that high power settings may be needed during taxi, additional time may be needed to allow the engine to warm up prior to taxi. Ideally this warm up period should be sufficient to allow the CHT, if fitted, to increase into the green range.
If the flight is being taken from an airfield where no taxi is possible (or only very short taxi) additional warm-up time should be allowed before take-off .

Taxi

Taxi speed should be limited to a brisk walk, the aircraft is is its most unstable condition on the ground, especially with strong winds that may reach minimum flying speeds.
Brake use should be kept to a minimum by anticipation of slowing down or stopping followed by reduction of power to idle prior to applying brakes. This keeps brake wear to a minimum and ensures brakes are at their most effective in case of a rejected takeoff.

Controls must be held to prevent buffeting by the wind and for the most desirable handling during taxi. Elevators should be held fully aft when taxiing over rough surfaces, bumps or gravel to reduce loads on the nose wheel and propeller damage. In all other cases the controls should be held with consideration of the wind for the best aerodynamic effects.

Flight control surfaces should be positioned to ensure the aircraft is not rocked or displaced and controls are not subjected to unnecessary forces by the prevailing wind.

The diagram below illustrates positions of controls in relation to the relative wind for aerodynamic effects.

The following phrase may be helpful as a memory aid:

CLIMB INTO wind, DIVE AWAY from the wind

That is, taxing into wind, pull back (climb) and turn towards the wind, taxing with the wind behind you, push forward (dive) and turn away from the wind.

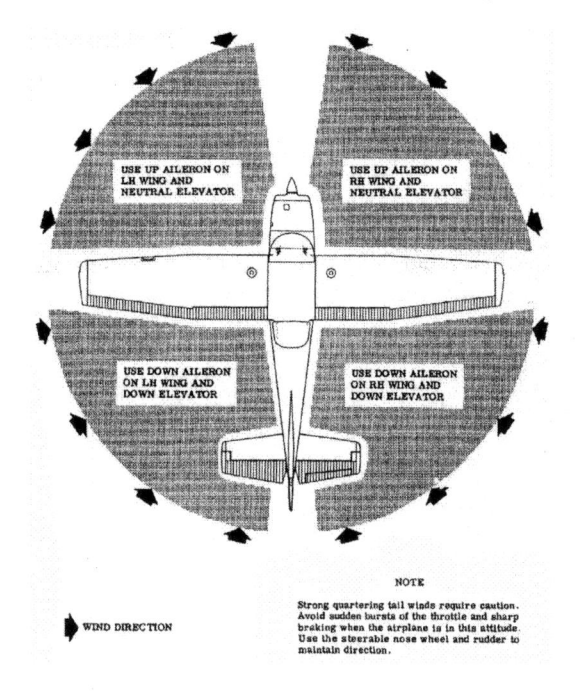

NOTE
Strong quartering tail winds require caution. Avoid sudden bursts of the throttle and sharp braking when the airplane is in this attitude. Use the steerable nose wheel and rudder to maintain direction.

If incorrectly positioned, a strong wind can lift the into wind wing, or the tail especially with the low flying speeds of the Cessna 152. These positions are designed to ensure the most positive, downwards force is available on the into wind flying surfaces.

Engine Run-up

The run-up and before takeoff checks are usually performed at the holding point. Ensure the aircraft is parked, where possible facing either into wind or in light winds towards the approach path, in a clear area away from debris, and with the propeller wash clear of other aircraft.

Advance the engine to 1700rpm, ensuring the brakes are holding firmly, and perform the following checks (note: some operations may require additional checks):

- ✈ Above 3000ft density altitude, the mixture should be leaned for takeoff. The following procedure may be used for leaning the mixture prior to takeoff:
    - Adjust the mixture till peak rpm is achieved, then enrich the mixture, approximately 3 rotations. This procedure is similar to that carried out enroute for leaning, however at 1700rpm the EGT will be too cool to use as a reference. This check may also be performed at lower altitudes to check correct operation and setting of the mixture, however the mixture should be returned to full rich before takeoff. *For maximum performance the mixture should be set at full power, however for all normal operations, where no other guidance is provided by the manufacturer, it is considered sufficient to set the mixture at 1700rpm.* Note: mixture setting is completed first since the other items are dependant on the engine operating at the correct mixture;
- ✈ Carburettor heat should be checked by pulling out the carburettor heat control knob for a brief period of time then returning to the cold position. The engine rpm should drop about 100rpm during the carburettor heat operation, from the less dense air, confirming the heat is working. Don't operate the carburettor heat for a prolonged period of time, because the heated air entering the engine is not filtered;
- ✈ A magneto check should be done as follows:
    - Move ignition switch first to L and note the rpm drop;
    - Then move the switch back to BOTH to clear the other set of plugs and regain the reference rpm;
    - Move the switch to R position, note the rpm drop and return the switch to BOTH position;
    - The rpm drop in either L or R position should not exceed 125 rpm and the difference between the drop on the L and R should be no greater than 50 rpm;
- ✈ Verify proper operation of the alternator and alternator warning light by selection of an electrical load, and confirm correct indications (in the green) of all engine gauges and the suction gauge;
- ✈ The DI may be checked and set against the compass at this point as the reading will be more accurate due to the effect of magnetic interference and suction pressure at 1700rpm than at 1000rpm;

✈ Reduce the engine rpm to idle to re-confirm correct idle operation, on the warm engine with the correct mixture setting. The engine should idle at approximately 500-700rpm. Then return to 1000 rpm for pre takeoff checks.

Pre Takeoff Vital Actions

The flight manual provides the "minimum required actions" before takeoff, generally there are some additional operational items to check. Many flight schools or operators will have their own check lists and/or acronyms for the pre take-off checks. Acronyms are highly recommended for single pilot operations. One of the most popular is as follows:

Too	Trims and controls tested set and checked, ensure trim set for takeoff and controls full and free movement.
Many	Mixture set for takeoff
	Magnetos on both
Pilots	Pitch fixed, pumps on (as applicable)
Go	Gills open (as applicable)
	Gyros uncaged and set
Fly	Fuel contents checked on correct tank, primer locked, pump as required,
	Flaps set for takeoff, 0 or 10 degrees
In	Instrument panel check from right to left, DI aligned with compass
Heaven	Hatches and harnesses secure
Early	Electrics circuit breakers checked, systems set

These flow checks should be followed up by a pre-takeoff checklist where available,

Takeoff

Takeoff is always carried out under full power with the heels on the floor to avoid accidental use of the toe brakes.

Unless on a gravel runway or with traffic on final approach oe asked to expedite by ATC, it is always good airmanship to line up straight on the runway centreline, stop and reset idle rpm, and complete final line up checks.

The following items should be selected and checked on line up, (these also have a helpful acronym):

REmember	Runway clear from obstruction,
	Engine parameters checked
What	Windsock aligned, controls into wind
To	Transponder on ALT
Do	DI aligned with compass and indicating runway direction
Last	Lights strobe and landing lights

It is important to check full-throttle engine operation early in the takeoff run. Any sign of rough engine operation or sluggish engine acceleration or less than expected takeoff power is cause to discontinue the takeoff. The engine should run smoothly and with constant static rpm of 2280 to 2380rpm.

When taking off from gravel runways, the throttle should be advanced slowly. This allows the aeroplane to start rolling before high rpm is developed as loose gravel is harmful to the propeller. On a rolling takeoff the gravel will be blown back of the propeller rather than pulled into it.

Keep the aircraft straight on the runway, and balanced during the climb with rudder (this will require right ruder due to the slipstream and torque effects).

In a normal takeoff, protect the nose-wheel by holding the weight of it during the roll, this will also assist with rotation.

Once airborne initially maintain a speed of 65kts, or best rate of climb, at a safe altitude, not below 300ft AGL, confirm the speed is above 60kts and retract the flaps if used, then complete the after takeoff checks.

→ The following are recommended **after takeoff checks (BUMPFFL)**:
- **Brakes** – ON and OFF;
- **Undercarriage** – FIXED;
- **Power / Pitch / Mixture** – SET;
- **Flaps** – UP;
- **Fuel Valve** – ON;
- **Engine's Temperature & Pressure** – CHECK;
- **Landing light** – OFF (or as required).

Wing Flaps Setting on Takeoff

Normal takeoff is accomplished with wing flaps in UP position. Using the flaps for takeoff will shorten ground roll but will reduce climb performance of aircraft.
However, during testing, it is established which flap settings will be most favourable and the associated performance is tabulated.
Using 10 degrees wing flaps on C152 reduces the total takeoff distance to 50ft obstacle clearance by approximately 10%.
Flap deflections greater than 10 degrees are not approved for takeoff.
If flaps are used for takeoff, they should not be retracted below 300ft AGL and a safe flap retraction speed of 60kts is reached, as on flaps retraction the aircraft loses lift and with insufficient speed may sink down.

Short Field Takeoff

On short field, the recommended technique specifies use of maximum power prior to brake release, 10 degrees wing flaps, a lift off speed of 50kts and an initial obstacle clearance climb speed of 54kts. Once obstacles are cleared, and a safe altitude reached, accelerate to complete the initial climb at the best rate of climb

speed, 67kts at sea level (see more about climb speeds under the Climb section below). Retract the flaps only after reaching a minimum speed of 60kt.
The figures from the flight manual of the aircraft you are flying must be referred to for operational purposes. Following the procedure specified in the flight manual will provide for the required runway length specified in the performance tables. Any deviation from the recommended procedure should be expected to give a decrease in performance, that is, require more runway length.

Soft Field Takeoff

Soft or rough field takeoffs are performed with the maximum flap setting permitted for takeoff, for the Cessna 152 this is 10 degrees. The aircraft should be lifted off the ground as soon as practical in a slightly tail-low attitude to reduce the large frictional drag caused by the runway surface. If no obstacles are ahead, the aeroplane should be immediately accelerated to an appropriate climb speed, normally to best rate of climb speed, 67kts at sea level. If there are obstacles, the aircraft should be accelerated to 54kts, the initial short field takeoff speed with 10 degrees of flap, and this speed should be maintained untill all obstacles are cleared.

Crosswind Component

The maximum demonstrated crosswind component is 12 knots, measured at a height of 33 feet. This is the highest value for which the aeroplane has been tested during takeoff and landings.
The maximum demonstrated crosswind is not a limitation, and as such is only listed in the normal operating section of the pilot's operating handbook, however, it is good practice to not exceed this speed until sufficient experience operating the aircraft safely under dual training in crosswind conditions has been gained. It is also vital that an inexperienced pilot should reduce this value even further, and many flight schools will impose additional cross wind limits on low time students.

Crosswind Takeoff

During a crosswind takeoff, as the aircraft becomes airborne, it will tend to move sideways with the air mass. At low speeds it may sink back onto ground with strong sideways movement which can damage the undercarriage or result in departure from the runway and loss of control. This effect is worst at low take-off speeds as the ratio of sideways to forward forces is higher.
The recommended technique is to hold the aeroplane firmly on the ground to slightly higher lift-off speed and then positively lift-off with a backward movement of the control column. Once airborne the aircraft nose is turned slightly into wind to prevent drift on climb-out, termed, 'crabbing into wind'. Ailerons should be held into wind, to prevent the into wind wing lifting early and assist in directional control. As the forward speed increases the amount of aileron can be reduced, and when at rotational speed ailerons must be neutral, to ensure a clean level rotation.

Climb

The normal climb with or without flap, is made at an airspeed of approximately 65 kts using full power. This speed is close to the 'maximum rate of climb' speed or 'Vy', which is used to reach cruise altitude as quickly as possible, as it gains the greatest altitude in a given time.
The best rate of climb speed for the C152 reduces with altitude, to retain the same wing angle as the TAS increases, and is 67kts at sea level, reducing to 61kts at 10,000ft.

When required to clear an obstacle, the recommended speed is 55kts, providing a 'maximum angle of climb' speed or 'Vx'. Vx gains the greatest altitude for a given horizontal distance, providing a lower rate of climb, but at a steeper angle.
Because the slow airspeed results in reduced engine cooling, higher engine temperatures, and a lower speed margin above the stall, it should be used only for short periods while clearing obstacles, thereafter acceleration to Vy should be commenced, to gain height quickly until reaching a safe altitude or approximately 1500ft.
Once at a safe altitude above ground, if sufficient performance allows, a cruise climb may be achieved by lowering the nose to maintain a rate of climb of 500ft/min, or an airspeed of 70 to 80kts.
Often with a heavy aircraft or high takeoff altitudes and temperatures, the aircraft will have insufficient climb performance to permit accelerating to speeds above Vy. For extended climbs at Vy, engine temperatures must be monitored carefully, and an intermediate level off may be needed for cooling purposes. These intermediate level offs can also be used for lookout, as visibility during the climb is obscured.

Cruise

Normal cruising is performed between 2200 to 2400rpm resulting in an indicated airspeed 90 to 105kts.

The normal operating power range for manoeuvring is from 1900 to 2550 rpm.

Mixture Setting

To achieve the best fuel consumption and engine operation, the mixture should be leaned during the cruise.
With an EGT gauge, the mixture should be set to approximately 50 to 100 degrees rich of peak. If no EGT gauge is available, the equivalent setting is approximately three turns rich of peak rpm.
When setting EGT, normally there is a reference needle provided on the gauge, which, once the peak is established should be set manually to reflect the peak. During flight the mixture setting may then be monitored with reference to the peak setting, ensuring it remains approximately 50 to 100 degrees below. Changes in ambient conditions may require a small adjustment or a full reset.

Cruise Checks

During the cruise it is important to have periodic aircraft status checks. These checks will not form part of a checklist, as they are considered normal flying duties and should be done regularly as part of good airmanship, however it is helpful to have an acronym to remind us what to check.

➢ One of the recommended cruise checks is defined by the acronym 'SAFDIE', as follows:
- **S – Suction** – CHECK;
- **A – Amps** – CHECK;
- **F – Fuel** – CHECK sufficient quantity and balanced;
- **D – DI** – ALIGNED with the compass;
- **I – Icing** – CHECK (carb heat/airframe);
- **E – Engine** – CHECK (temperature and pressure, mixture).

Approach and Landing

The recommended speed range for a normal approach is 60 to 70kts flaps up and 55 to 65kts flaps down. During initial training, the minimum speed is usually increased by 5 knots, that is 65-70 flaps up and 60-65kts flaps down, to provide a bigger safety margin above the stall speed.

In windy conditions, a wind correction factor should also be applied increasing the safety margin to allow for wind shear.

The rule for application of the wind and gust factor is:
➢ ½ HWC and all of the gust

For example, with a wind of 20kts gusting 30 at 60 degrees to the runway center line, the HWC is 10kts and the gust is 10kts so the wind should be increased by 20kts.

Although this sounds like a large increase in speed the following must be remembered, only head wind component must be considered and as only half is taken there is still a reduction in distance from the reduced ground speed, as landing calculations should be made in still wind.

Headwind component can be calculated from graphs, trigonometry or on request from ATC.

When the wind is gusting there is generally a significant headwind factor so even if all gust is taken landing distance may not be significantly affected, and whenever the wind is reported gusting, particularly at altitude we need to have all the resources available to deal with unknown influence of windshear, especially with a light training aircraft where only small amounts of residual power available for recovery.

The rule however is a starting point and may be modified as required for conditions and field length.

Carburettor heat should be applied for low power operation on approach, and selected cold, on short final for possible go around or ground operations.

Short Field Landing

For a short field operation, the recommended technique is for a final approach speed of 54kts with 30 degrees of flap. This speed may be achieved any time after selection of full flap on final approach, but should be stabilised by not lower than 200ft above the ground. Positive control of the approach speed and descent should be made to ensure accuracy of the touchdown point. Power may be reduced to idle once obstacles are cleared, and the landing should be made positively on the main wheels, nose high, and as close as possible to the stall. Thereafter gently lower the nosewheel and apply maximum braking, or braking as required by the field length.

It is important to remember with a short field landing, the speed on touchdown has as much to do with the landing distance used as the touch down point. An aircraft should never be 'forced' onto the ground, as this will result in a longer roll out, and may cause a bounce or nose-wheel contact. If the touchdown point has been misjudged, it is better to initiate a go around than to try to land the aircraft at a higher speed.

Crosswind Landing

When approaching to land with a crosswind the aircraft flight manual discusses crabbed, slipping or combination method.

Whenever there is a crosswind during flight, to prevent drift while maintaining balanced flight, the aircraft must be crabbed into wind as detailed above for crosswind takeoff, otherwise the aircraft would be continuously blown off track.
For landing, the aircraft nose must be brought in line with the runway, to prevent side loads on the tyres and to aid in directional control. In doing so the aircraft will begin to drift, and the 'into wind' wing will need to be lowered just enough to keep the aircraft on the runway centre line. In this situation, the 'into wind' wheel will make contact first, followed by the remaining main wheel, and last the nose wheel should be positively placed on the ground. Once all three wheels are on the ground, the ailerons are placed into wind to prevent aerodynamic side forces lifting the into wind wing, ensuring positive directional control.
The question of differing techniques, on conventional aircraft, is therefore only a question of when to transition from the 'crabbed' approach to the landing configuration.
This is ideally achieved as late as possible, that is during the round out, because flying in the wing down results in a slipped, unbalanced condition, which is uncomfortable and adds considerable drag and reduced controllability. During training, while learning to become familiar with cross wind landing techniques, transition into the 'slipped' condition may be commenced earlier, during the intermediate part of the final approach, to assist the student with learning the degree of control input to apply during a phase of lower workload.

In a strong crosswind a slightly higher approach speed may be required to maintain more effective control against the wind factor. A slightly higher touchdown speed is also recommended to prevent drift in the transition between effective aerodynamic control and effective nose wheel steering.

Reduction in flap setting improves lateral stability, and a flapless or reduced flap landing may also be considered to assist in control during strong crosswinds.
It should be noted the C152 is quite controllable with full flap, well in excess of the maximum demonstrated crosswind, and this a good exercise to practise with an instructor.

Flapless Landing

Two items of importance should be considered for a flapless landing.
- ✦ Lack of drag to assist with the descent and approach;
- ✦ The increased stall speed with flap up compared to the normal landing configuration.

To assist with overcoming these items a slightly lower power setting and higher approach speed should be used. If necessary the downwind may be extended slightly. Due to these factors the approach and round out will be flatter than for a normal approach, and the aircraft may tend to float during the flare, requiring a longer hold off.

Balked Landing

On a 'go-round' manoeuvre, full power should be applied, and the wing flaps reduced to 20 degrees immediately thereafter. There is no limiting speed for reduction of the flaps from 30 to 20, as this is mainly drag flap, and needs to be actioned to ensure the aircraft achieves a positive climb out path after power application. The initial target speed for clearing obstacles is 55kts.

Upon reaching a safe altitude and airspeed, the flaps should be retracted in stages to the full UP position.

The flight manual permits retraction of flaps 'slowly' at 55kts for a balked landing, however on takeoff, retraction of flap from 10 degrees to 0 requires a minimum speed of 60kts. To be on the safe side, it is recommended to apply a minimum speed of 60kts for further flap retraction in both cases, unless performance is extremely critical. Weight, density altitude and turbulence, will play a role in this decision.

After Landing Checks

When clearing the runway after landing, it is vital to complete the after landing checks for engine management and airmanship considerations.

The mixture which has been set rich for the go-around, should be leaned for taxi to prevent spark plug fowling. The wing flaps must be retracted (to prevent ATC suspecting a hijacking has occurred!), it is polite to select the strobe and landing lights off and the transponder should be selected to standby, unless otherwise dictated by ATC procedures.

After Landing checks can be completed in a flow pattern followed by a check-list, or as a check list where available.

✈ Typical after landing checks are as follows:
- **Cowl Flaps** – FIXED;
- **Mixture** – SET for taxi;
- **Flaps** – UP;
- **Strobes and Landing Light** – OFF;
- **Transponder** – STANDBY.

Taxi and Shutdown

Taxi should be planned to suit engine cooling requirements when needed. If you are operating on rough gravel remember to avoid needing to operate the aircraft stationary at idle for prolonged periods.

In a normally aspirated engine, providing the approach was accomplished without using excessive amounts of power, in most cases the taxi should provide sufficient time for cooling down the engine.

Before completing the shutdown, it may be desired to complete a dead-cut check to ensure all magneto positions, in particular the OFF position is working, so the propeller is not left 'live'.

Shutdown again can then be accomplished in a flow pattern, followed up with a checklist where available.

✈ Typical shutdown checks are as follows:
- **Avionics** – OFF;
- **Mixture** – CUTOFF;
- **Magnetos** – OFF;
- **Master** – OFF;
- **Control Lock** – IN;
- **Flight Time/Hour Metre** – RECORDED;
- **Tie Downs/Screens/Covers** – FITTED.

Circuit Pattern

The standard circuit pattern, unless published otherwise, is the left circuit pattern at 1000ft above ground for piston engine aeroplanes.

The circuit pattern may differ from airport to airport. Ask your instructor, the briefing office or consult the relevant aeronautical information publication for the pattern on your airfield.

The circuit pattern contains all the critical manoeuvres required for a normal flight, condensed into a short space of time. It is a great way to learn the critical flight checks, practice manoeuvres and improve overall flying skills.

Note: The following provides guidelines for all the checks required during flight. Some checks have been repeated here to provide a complete study aid to assist students in learning the procedures. Full details of each phase are contained in the relevant parts of the preceding pages in this section.

CESSNA 152 TRAINING MANUAL

The following summarises in-flight procedures for circuit patterns from start up to shutdown:

→ Complete the aircraft preflight walk-around, ensuring fuel and oil quantities are sufficient, all required equipment is serviceable, and the condition of the aircraft and all components is acceptable for flight, complete the cockpit set up and the before start checks.
- **Preflight Inspection** – COMPLETE;
- **Tach/Hobbs/Time** – RECORDED;
- **Passenger Briefing** – COMPLETE;
- **Brakes** – SET/HOLD;
- **Doors** – CLOSED;
- **Seats / Seatbelts** – ADJUSTED, LOCKED;
- **Fuel Selector Valve** – BOTH/CORRECT TANK;
- **Cowl Flaps** – OPEN;
- **Undercarriage** – FIXED;
- **Magnetos** – BOTH;
- **Avionics** – OFF;
- **Electrical Equipment** – OFF;
- **Rotating Beacon** – ON.

→ Once ready to start complete the 'ready for start' or 'cleared for start' checks;
- **Circuit Breakers** – CHECK IN;
- **Mixture** – RICH / AS REQUIRED;
- **Prime** – AS REQUIRED (1 to 3 as required);
- **Throttle** – SET approx ½ centimetre;
- **Propeller Area** – CLEAR.

→ Start the engine, complete the after start flows, and complete the after start and pre-taxi checks;
- **Mixture** – SET for taxi;
- **Magnetos** – CHECKED;
- **Engine Instruments** – CHECKED;
- **Flaps** – RETRACTED/SET FOR TAKEOFF;
- **Transponder** – STANDBY/GROUND.
-

→ Test the brakes as soon as possible after the aircraft begins moving, at any convenient time during the taxi check the flight and navigation instruments, then complete the taxi checks.
- **Brakes** – CHECKED;
- **Avionics and Flight Instruments** – CHECKED/SET;
- **Nav Instruments** – TESTED/CHECKED/SET.

→ Taxi towards the runway in use and position the aircraft clear of the holding point to carry out the **engine run-up** and pre takeoff checks. Prior to the run-up ensure that:
- The slipstream will not affect other aircraft;

- A brake failure will not cause you to run into other aircraft or obstacles;
- Loose stones will not damage the propeller.

→ Set the park brake and complete the **Engine Run-up:**
- **Power** – SET 1700rpm;
- **Mixture** – SET for elevation (above 3000ft density altitude);
- **Magnetos** – CHECK left, both, right, both, confirm smooth operation within limits for drop and differences;
- **Engine's Temperature & Pressure** – CHECK;
- **Ammeter** – CHECK under load;
- **Suction** – CHECK green;
- **DI** – ALIGNED with compass;
- **Power** – reduce to idle, and confirm steady idle at around 500 to 700rpm, return to 1000rpm.

→ Complete the **Pre Takeoff Vital Actions:**
- **Trims and Controls** – TESTED, SET AND CHECKED, confirm trims set for takeoff, and controls full and free movement;
- **Mixture** – SET for takeoff,
- **Magnetos** – BOTH;
- **Pitch** – FIXED;
- **Gills** *(Cowls)* – *FIXED* ;
- **Gyros** – CHECKED and SET;
- **Fuel** – CHECKED: Contents sufficient, on correct tank, primer locked, pump as required (normally off for Cessna high wing aircraft),
- **Flaps** – Set for takeoff;
- **Instruments** – CHECKED and SET: Panel check from right to left, DI aligned with compass, check clock, note time;
- **Hatches and harnesses** – SECURE;
- **Electrics** – CHECKED, circuit breakers checked, systems set.

→ Consider air traffic control and radio procedures, and review traffic to ensure the final approach is clear before lining up on the runway.
Line up and ensure that the nose wheel is straight (make full use of the runway length available) and perform line-up check:
- **Runway** – UNOBSTRUCTED, correct vector, and heading aligned;
- **Engine** – CHECKED, Temperatures, pressures green;
- **Windsock** – Check direction and strength (confirm against ATC wind), position control column accordingly;
- **Transponder** ALT (TA/RA or ON);
- **DI** – ALIGNED with compass and reading runway bearing;
- **Landing Light and Transponder** – ON.

→ Takeoff and climb maintaining runway alignment. Upon reaching a safe altitude (300' above airfield elevation), accelerate to best rate of climb speed and at a minimum of 60kts raise the flaps (if used);

→ Perform the **after takeoff check (BUMPFFL)**:
- **Brakes** – ON and OFF;
- **Undercarriage** – FIXED;
- **Power / Pitch / Mixture** – SET;
- **Flaps** – UP;
- **Fuel Valve** – ON;
- **Engine's Temperature & Pressure** – CHECK;
- **Landing Light** – OFF.

→ At a minimum of 500' scan the area into which you will be turning and then turn onto crosswind leg using a normal climbing turn (bank 15° or Rate 1 maximum).

→ Reaching circuit height, level-off, allow the speed to settle, set downwind power, approx 2300rpm, and trim the aeroplane for straight-and-level flight.

→ Scan the area into which you will be turning and turn onto downwind leg, selecting a reference point well ahead on which to parallel the runway.

→ Circuit width should be approximately 1½ to 2 miles from the runway.

→ When abeam the runway, make ATC call and perform **downwind check (BUMPFFEL)**:
- **Brakes** – ON and OFF;
- **Undercarriage** – FIXED;
- **Power / Pitch / Mixture** – SET;
- **Flaps** – UP;
- **Fuel Valve** – ON;
- **Engine's Temperature & Pressure** – CHECK;
- **Landing Light** – ON.

→ Just before base leg (45° to the runway), check that speed not exceeding Vfe and lower flap to 10°.

→ After scanning for traffic on Base and Final, turn base leg performing standard medium turn to the left.

→ After levelling the wings, select Carb. Heat on, reduce power to 1700 RPM (while keeping the nose up for the approach speed), lower the flaps to 20° and commence descent.

→ Trim the aeroplane to maintain approximately 65-70kts and use power to maintain the desired approach angle.

→ Visually check the final approach clear of traffic and anticipate the turn to final so as to roll out with the aircraft aligned with the direction of the landing runway and no less then 500'.

→ Lower the flaps to full position, reduce to the required final approach speed, and complete **before landing check (CCUMP)**:
- **Cowl Flaps** – FIXED;
- **Carburettor Heat** – COLD;
- **Undercarriage** – FIXED;
- **Mixture** – SET for go around power;

- **Pitch** – FIXED.
→ Execute the appropriate landing procedure.
→ Maintain the centre line during the landing run by using rudder and wings kept level with aileron. Brakes may be used once the nose-wheel is on the ground.

→ Once clear of the runway, stop the aeroplane, set 1000 RPM and complete **after landing check**:
- **Cowl Flaps** – FIXED;
- **Mixture** – SET for taxi;
- **Flaps** – UP;
- **Strobes and Landing Light** – OFF;
- **Transponder** – STANDBY.

Taxi to the parking area and complete the shut down flows and **shut down check**:
- **Avionics** – OFF;
- **Mixture** – CUTOFF;
- **Magnetos** – OFF;
- **Master** – OFF;
- **Control Lock** – IN;
- **Flight Time/Hour Metre** – RECORDED;
- **Tie Downs/Screens/Covers** – FITTED.

Note on Checklists

Present standard and recommended operating practice on a single-pilot aeroplane dictate use of a checklist AFTER completion of vital actions in a flow pattern on each critical stage of the flight, such as before and after takeoff, on downwind and final leg.
The acronyms above therefore provide a memory aid to allow for completion of the checks prior to reading the checklist.

Acronyms are strongly recommended for single pilot, light aircraft operations to avoid memory related errors. Ideally they should be as generic as possible to avoid error patterns when changing between aircraft models and types, which happens more frequently in light aircraft. For this reason items such as undercarriage, pitch, and cowl flaps have been left in the memory checks included herein, since these items are both critical and most easily forgotten. Note however, these items should not be on a checklist, as only applicable items are included on a checklist. Any convenient acronym is acceptable providing the minimum required items are catered for, and since it is a memory aid prior to completing the aircraft operator's checklist (or your own checklist if one is not provided), they can be personalised to meet the individual pilot's requirements.

The approved Pilot's Operating Handbook provides a checklist of minimum items which must be adhered to, it is often good practice to include a number of additional items, a checklist can then be developed to assist with completion of mandatory and critical items. Any suitable checklist may be used providing it does not omit any required items from the POH, although it is always best to have a checklist specifically written for the aircraft, specific to the type, model and serial number and inclusive of any equipment, engine or airframe modifications.

For single pilot operations, a hands free checklist is recommended for in flight checks. Alternatively consideration should be made of omitting checklists during critical phases, since the benefit of the checklist is outweighed by the distraction of performing it.

The above checks and procedures are based on standard training practices, including all the relevant items from C152 Pilot's Operating Handbook, and can be modified to suit a specific operation.

Checks for emergencies and must be memorized and are sometimes followed up by a "do-list" accomplished in a read and do manner. See next section on emergencies in the C152.

EMERGENCY PROCEDURES

The main consideration in any emergency should be given to flying the aircraft. Primary attention should be given to altitude and airspeed control and thereafter to the emergency solution.
Rapid and proper handling of an emergency will be useless if the aircraft is stalled and impacts with the ground due to loss of control. This is most critical during takeoff, approach and landing.
The checklists in this section should be used as a guide only. The emergency checklist and procedures for your particular aircraft model specified in the aircraft Pilots Operating Handbook should be consulted for operational purposes.

Emergency During Takeoff

Any emergency or abnormality during takeoff calls for the takeoff to be aborted. The most important action is to attempt to stop the aeroplane safely on the remaining runway. Once the aircraft is safely stopped, consideration should be made of securing the aircraft (fuel, ignition and electrics) and evacuation if required.

After the aircraft is airborne, re-landing should be considered only if sufficient runway is available for this purpose. As a general rule, the runway is sufficient, if the end of the runway can be seen clearly in front of the aircraft. Where no sufficient runway is available, the engine failure after takeoff procedure should be followed.

Engine Failure after Takeoff

The recommended gliding speed is 60kts. This is also the speed recommended in case of an engine failure after takeoff.
Prompt lowering of the nose to maintain airspeed and establish a glide attitude is the first response to an engine failure after takeoff.
Landing should be planned straight ahead, within an arc or ±30 degrees to either side. Turns, if required, should be made with no more than 15 degrees angle of bank. Any increase in bank angle or angle of turn will result in increased height loss or an increased chance of stalling or both, and have often resulted in unnecessary fatalities.

The procedures in the pilot's operating handbook assume that adequate time exists after selection of a landing site, to secure the fuel, ignition, and electrical system, and open doors prior to touchdown. These actions are required to prevent post crash fire and to assist in evacuation, however at very low altitudes there may be only enough time to concentrate on the landing itself.

Any attempt to restart the engine depends on altitude available, and if altitude is available, the procedure should be considered as an 'engine failure in flight'.
A controlled descent and crash landing on an unprepared surface is more preferable to uncontrolled impact with the ground in the attempted engine start.

Just before the landing:
- **Airspeed** – 60kts
This speed gives the best gliding distance with a propeller windmilling and flaps in up position.
- **Mixture** – IDLE CUT-OFF
- **Fuel selector** – OFF;
This will ensure that the engine will be cut-off from the fuel system and thus minimise fire possibility after an impact.
- **Ignition switch** - OFF;
- **Master switch** – OFF
The master switch should be switched off after the flaps being set in the desired position, to minimize the chance of a fire after touchdown.
- **Doors** - UNLOCKED
The doors should be unlocked in aid of rapid evacuation after the touchdown.

After landing:
- Stop the aeroplane;
- Check that fuel, ignition and electronics are OFF;
- Evacuate as soon as possible.

Gliding and Forced Landing

For a forced landing without engine power a gliding speed of 65 kts should be used, this allows for increased performance in case of deviation below planned speed and provides more penetration into wind over a longer distance.
- ✈ The first priority is to establish the glide speed and turn toward the suitable landing area;
- ✈ While gliding toward the area, an effort should be made to identify the cause of the failure;
- ✈ Ensure a Mayday call is given before too much height and time is lost;
- ✈ An engine restart should be attempted as shown in the checklist below. If the attempts to restart the engine fail, focus on completing the forced landing without power. (Further attempts to restart distract the pilot from performing the forced landing procedure).
- ✈ Once committed to the forced landing procedure, secure the engine in preparation for landing;
- ✈ If the cause of engine failure is a mechanical failure or fire, the engine may be secured immediately and no restart should be attempted;
- ✈ Passengers must be briefed when time permits;
- ✈ On final approach, with full flap, the master switch should be turned off and the doors opened.

If the failure is partial, resulting in reduced or intermittent running, it is recommended to use the partial power till arrival overhead the intended area of landing, and then reduce to idle for the approach.

Once landing is assured, the engine should be secured. If a partial power setting is used and power is suddenly regained and lost again at a critical stage of approach, this may change the gliding ability of the aircraft making it will be impossible to reach the intended landing area safely. Additionally if the landing area is unprepared, it is best to have the engine secure prior to touchdown. Individual judgement is required depending on the circumstances.

Forced Landing Procedure:
✈ Primary actions
- Trim for 65kts (recommended forced landing speed);
- Carb heat on;
- Select a field, plan the approach.

✈ Finding the fault:
- **Fuel selector** – CHECK ON;
- **Mixture** – FULLY RICH*;
- **Carb. Heat** – PULL;
  One of the causes of an engine failure can be carburettor ice. By applying the Carb.heat, the problem can be eliminated.
- **Throttle** – FULLY FORWARD;
- **Ignition** – CHECK BOTH/L and R;
- **Primer** – IN AND LOCKED.

*Note: Mixture is recommended to be set rich in the pilots operating handbook, however if it is suspected the cut is from too rich setting at altitude, leaning can be opted for.

✈ Securing the engine:
- **Mixture** – IDLE CUT-OFF
- **Fuel selector** – OFF;
  This will ensure that the engine will be cut-off from the fuel system and thus minimise fire possibility after an impact.
- **Throttle** – FULLY FORWARD;
  By opening the throttle all the fuel left in the carburettor will be sucked out, and the fire possibility will be minimised.
- **Ignition switch** – OFF;
- **Master switch** – OFF
  The master switch should be switched off after the flaps being set in the desired position, and is done to minimize an electrical fire.
- **Doors** – UNLOCKED
  The doors should be unlatched in anticipation of a quick evacuation after the touchdown. After landing the same procedure as detailed for an engine failure after takeoff above, should be initiated.

In case of simulated forced landing training, the carburettor heat should be selected before closing the throttle. During an extended glide, select a partial power for a brief period every 500-1000ft to provide engine warming and to ensure power is available.

Engine Fire

In case of fire on the ground, the engine should be shut down immediately and fire must be controlled as quickly as possible.
In flight such emergency calls for execution of a forced landing. Do not attempt to restart the engine.
The pilot may initiate a sideslip to keep the flame away from the occupants. This procedure can be also used to extinguish the fire.

If required, the emergency descent may be initiated to land as soon as possible. Opening the window or door may produce a low pressure in the cabin and thus draw the fire into the cockpit. Therefore, all doors and windows should be kept closed till short final, where the door should be open in anticipation of a quick evacuation after the landing.

An engine fire is usually caused by fuel leak, an electrical short, or exhaust leak. If an engine fire occurs, the first step is to shut-off the fuel supply to the engine by putting the mixture to idle cut off and fuel valve to the off position. The ignition switch should be left on and throttle fully open in order for the engine to use the remaining fuel in the lines and carburettor.

The following check list should be used in quick and proper manner.

- During an engine start on ground:
  - **Cranking** – CONTINUE FOR A FEW MINUTES
    This will suck the flames and burning fuel through the carburettor into the engine. The fire may burn out of exhaust for a few minutes and extinguish if continue cranking.
  - **If engine starts - power** – 1700 rpm FOR A FEW MINUTES;
  - **Mixture** – IDLE CUT OFF
  - **Fuel valve** – CLOSED
  - **Ignition switch** – OFF
  - **Master switch** - OFF
    Use the fire extinguisher if the fire persists. Do not restart and call for maintenance for the engine inspection.

- In flight:
  - **Mixture** – IDLE CUT-OFF
  - **Fuel valve** – OFF;
  - **Throttle** – FULLY OPEN;
  - **Master switch** – OFF;
  - **Cabin Heat and Air** – OFF (To prevent the fire to be drawn into the cockpit).
  - **Airspeed** – 85kts If the fire is not extinguished, increase to a glide speed which may extinguish the fire.
  - **Forced landing** – EXECUTE

Electrical Fire

The indication of an electrical fire is usually the distinct odour of burning insulation. Once an electrical fire is detected, attempt to identify the effected circuit and equipment. If the affected circuit cannot be identified or isolated, switch the master switch off, thus removing the possible source of the fire.
If the affected circuit or equipment is identified, isolate the circuit by pulling out the applicable circuit breaker and switching the equipment off.

Smoke may be removed by opening the windows and the cabin air control.
However, if the fire or smoke increases, the windows and cabin air control should be closed.
The fire extinguisher may be used, if required.
Ventilate the cockpit after that to remove the gases.
Landing should be initiated as soon as practical on the first suitable airfield.
If the fire cannot be extinguished, land as soon as possible.

Stalling and Spinning

There is no pronounced aerodynamic stall warning (buffet). Stall warning is indicated by a steady audible signal 10 kts before the actual stall is reached and remains on until the flight attitude is changed. The stall characteristics are conventional for flaps retracted and extended. Slight elevator buffeting may occur just before the stall with flaps down.

Spin characteristics are normal. To enter the spin, full rudder should be applied about 10kts before stall and stick held fully back. A positive wing drop may occur if the aircraft is unbalanced or can be induced by the use of partial power at the entry.
The throttle should be closed on spin entry.
Intentional spins with flaps extended are prohibited, this is mainly because the high speed which may occur during recovery is potentially damaging to the flaps/wing structure.

Rough Running Engine

A rough engine running can be caused by a number of different reasons, faults that can be dealt with from the cockpit include spark plug fouling, magneto faults, a blocked air intake, and carburettor ice. Engine faults causing rough running will normally be associated with changes in oil pressure and temperature, although in this case the fault cannot be fixed, the situation can be managed to achieve the most desirable outcome. See the relevant sections following regarding each of these faults.

Magneto Faults

A sudden engine roughness or misfiring is often an indication of a magneto fault. Switching from BOTH to the L or R position will confirm if one magneto is faulty, and identify which one. In this situation, take care with switching, as if one magneto has grounded or failed completely, no change will occur when selecting the working magneto and a complete power loss will occur when the failed magneto is selected.

Spark Plug Faults

A slight engine roughness can be caused by one or more spark plugs becoming fouled. This often occurs during prolonged operation at low power settings with the mixture set too rich, and commonly happens at high density altitudes during taxi, well below 3000ft pressure altitude where Cessna recommends leaning the mixture.

Switching to one magneto can normally isolate the problem, as running the cylinder on one plug will cause misfiring on the cylinder that contains the faulty plug. (This is the same procedure used when an excessive magneto drop or rough running is experienced during the engine run-up prior to departure). As with magneto faults, care should be taken when applying this procedure in-flight, as if fouling is severe enough to affect more than one cylinder, it is possible that there could be a severe loss of power or engine cut when switching to one plug.

If the fault is due to fouling, leaning the mixture to peak or just rich of peak and running at a moderate power setting for a few minutes to burn off the excessive carbon should fix the problem. This procedure often needs to be performed during the engine run-up, where plug fouling has occurred during taxi or while standing for a long period. Note that it is not recommended to operate at peak with more than 55% power, however there may be cases where more power is needed, care should be taken to monitor the cylinder temperatures.

If the problem persists after several minutes operation at the correct mixture setting, it is likely to be caused by a faulty spark plug which must be replaced. Continue to operate on BOTH, or if extreme roughness dictates selection of the L or R position, select the L or R magneto and continue to the nearest suitable airfield.

Abnormal Oil Pressure or Temperature

Low oil pressure, which is not accompanied by high oil temperature, may indicate a failure of the gauge or the relief valve. This is not necessarily cause for an immediate precautionary landing, but a landing at the nearest suitable airfield should be planned for inspection. The situation should be closely monitored for any changes.

A partial or complete loss of oil pressure, accompanied by a rise in oil temperature is good reason to suspect an engine failure is imminent. Select a suitable field for a precautionary or forced landing. Reduce engine power as far as possible and plan to use minimum power for the approach. If possible plan a glide approach to allow for continuation in the event of a complete engine failure.

A small reduction in oil pressure with a rise in temperature is normal, since the viscosity of the oil will change as the temperature increases.

Any increase in oil temperature without a clear cause is a sign of an impending engine problem. Attempts must be made to reduce the oil temperature and demands on the engine. Provisions should be made for the situation getting worse. Adjust your track towards areas more suitable for a forced landing, and consider suitable airfields for diversion or areas to complete a precautionary landing.

High engine temperatures which result from engine operations, for example during an extended climb, or prolonged operations at high power in high ambient temperatures, must also be monitored. If temperatures begin to approach the top of the green range, an attempt to increase cooling must be made, for example level off at an intermediate altitude, richen the mixture, reduce power or increase the airspeed, as available to the situation.

Blocked Air Intake

A blocked air intake is normally caused by a build up of debris or ice on the air filter. If the air intake becomes blocked, a partial or complete engine failure will result, depending on the degree of blockage. Although there is no alternate intake air, a blocked air intake can be resolved by selection of the carb. heat, since the carburettor heat bypasses the normal filtered intake, and provides an alternate supply of air to the engine. See further below about operation with carb. heat.

Carburettor Ice

Carburettor ice can be experienced during low rpm operation, but may also be experienced at normal cruise in the right conditions of humidity and temperature. Typically carburettor ice will form at humidities above 50% and temperatures from -10 to +25 degrees Celsius. In these conditions it is recommended to regularly, for example every 15 minutes with cruise checks, apply carb. heat for several seconds to prevent ice build up before the effects of loss of performance are felt. At temperatures approaching -10 and below, use of carb. heat can increase the temperature into the freezing range, and should be only used if icing is suspected. Carb. heat should not be used above 75% power, since it is extremely unlikely to experience carb. ice at these power settings, and the loss of power and additional heat are detrimental to the high engine demands.

The symptoms of carburettor ice build up are rough running, a drop in rpm, or severe icing may cause a complete power loss. Carburettor ice can be removed through immediate application of carburettor heat, by pulling the carb. heat knob. If there is icing, application of carb. heat may initially make the situation worse, avoid the temptation to close the carb. heat again, as this is normally a sign the ice is clearing.

Since the heated air causes a richer air/fuel mixture, the mixture setting may need to be readjusted if the carburettor heat is required to be used for any prolonged period, for example in a long low power descent. Remember to richen the mixture again prior to closing the carb. heat.

PERFORMANCE

Performance Specifications and Limitations

Performance figures given at 1670lbs (MAUW) and speeds in KIAS unless specified otherwise.

Structural Limitations

Gross weight (take-off and landing)		1670 lbs
Maximum ramp weigh weight		1675 lbs
		(5 lbs allowed for taxi fuel)
Basic empty weights	C152	1100-1115
(approximate)	C152 II	1130-1150
Baggage allowance		120 lbs (54kgs)
Flight load factor	Flaps up	+4.4g – -1.76g
Flight load factor	Flaps down	+3.5g – 0
Aerobat flight load factors	Flaps up	+6g – -3g
Aerobat flight load factors	Flaps down	+3.5g – 0

Engine

Engine (Lycoming O-235 series) power	108 or 110 hHP at 2550 rpm
Oil capacity	6 Qt maximum (4 min)
Usable fuel	24.5 USG (93 litres)
Main wheel tyre pressure	29 psi
Nose wheel tyre pressure	21 psi

Speeds

Never Exceed Speed (Vne)	149 kts (red line)
Maximum structural speed (Vno)	111 kts (top of green arc)
Maximum flap extended speed (Vfe)	85 kts (top of white arc)
Stall speed clean/cruise configuration (Vs)	40 kts (bottom of green arc)
Stall speed in landing configuration (Vso)	35 kts
Maximum demonstrated crosswind component	12 kts
Maximum maneuvering speed (Va)	104 kts at 1670lbs
	98kts at 1500lbs
	93kts at 1350lbs

Speeds for Normal Operation

Normal take-off climb out speed	65-70kts
Short field take off, Flaps 10°	lift off 50ft, 50ft 54kts
Best rate of climb speed	67-61kts, sea level to 10,000ft
Normal approach flaps 30°	55-65 kts
Normal approach flaps up	60-70 kts
Short field landing flaps 30°qq	54kts

Speeds for Emergency Operation

Engine failure after take-off	60 kts
Forced landing	65 kts flap up, 60 flap down
Precautionary landing	60 kts flap 20°, 55 kts full flap

Cruise Performance*
Cruise at 2000ft pressure altitude   2300 rpm 97KTAS, 5.4gph/ lts
Cruise at 10,000ft pressure altitude   2300 rpm 93KTAS, 4.5gph/ lts

*Cruise figures provided from the pilots operating handbook should be used with a contingency factor, a block cruises speed and fuel flow that allows for contingency and climb and descent are normally applied.

Ground Planning

Provided below is an example for completion of pre-flight performance planning. Weight and balance graphs and performance tables are found in the C152 POH, and pre-flight planning forms similar to the ones provided here, should be available at your local flying school.
Blank copies of performance worksheets used in these examples are available at http://www.redskyventures.org.

In this example, the aircraft needs to carry two pilots, 20 pounds of baggage, and sufficient fuel to fly 1.5 hours en route at 8000ft on a private flight under visual flight rules.

Navigation Planning

The first step in any flight planning is to determine the route, this is normally carried out on a navigation worksheet, then transferred to the flight log for use in flight.

An example of a navigation worksheet is shown below.

FM	TO	Alt	Temp	W/V	IAS	TAS	Trk T	Var.	Trk M	G/S	Dist	EET
TOTALS												

The navigation log may be completed very accurately with reported conditions, approximately with forecast conditions, or used with block figures and still wind during advance planning, where small adjustments can be applied later. In all cases contingency needs to be applied for unexpected conditions, since weather is never static.

Fuel Planning

After completion of the navigation log, or once we have determined the maximum expected flight time, the next step is to calculate the fuel required. How much load we can carry is dependent on the minimum required fuel, which in turn is dependant on the maximum expected flight time.

On the following page is an example of a CRUISE PERFORMANCE table from the performance section of the C152 POH. This table is provided for the purposes of demonstrating the required calculations, the table should _not_ be used for flight planning. The process described refers to the fuel planning worksheet on the subsequent page.

For the flight we will use an outside temperature of 20ºC above standard temperature, or -1 degrees Celsius at 8000ft. At 55% of power we should obtain a TAS of 93kts and a fuel consumption of 4.5 gallons per hour. Using the conversion factors given in the beginning of this manual 1USG = 3.785Lt we will in theory achieve 17 litres per hour fuel consumption. This figure is however in ideal conditions with the engine and airframe producing exactly the performance it achieved during testing.

To allow for power variations in climb and provide a more conservative approach a "block" figure of 25 litres per hour may be used for planning purposes. Using this figure for a 1.5 hour of flight we will require 37.5 litres of fuel.

In this example the fuel planning sheet is filled in as follows:
- On the first line enter the calculated amount of trip fuel in the fuel planning table as en route fuel, in our case 37.5 litres;
- On the second line enter 10% of this amount as contingency fuel, in our case 3.75 litres;
- Calculate and enter 45 minutes at the block consumption of 25lt/hr for VFR reserve, a total of 19 litres.

Add together all of the above, with the standard figures provided for unusable fuel (based on 6lt/1.5USG for the C152, and 3lt for taxi/takeoff fuel), and we find the minimum fuel required for the flight is 69 litres.

The fuel in the tanks should be checked to ensure more than the minimum required, if more the actual dipped fuel must be used, if less the aircraft must be fuelled to the minimum required. To use fuel quantity in weight and balance calculation, we shall convert fuel volume into the weight. Using the formula in the table, we will find 70 litres dipped is equivalent to 100 pounds of usable fuel (unusable fuel is allowed for in the aircraft weight). This figure can now be transferred to the weight and balance sheet.

CESSNA 152 TRAINING MANUAL

CRUISE PERFORMANCE

CONDITIONS:
1670 Pounds
Recommended Lean Mixture (See Section 4, Cruise)

NOT FOR OPERATIONAL USE

NOTE:
Cruise speeds are shown for an airplane equipped with speed fairings which increase the speeds by approximately two knots.

PRESSURE ALTITUDE FT	RPM	20°C BELOW STANDARD TEMP %BHP	KTAS	GPH	STANDARD TEMPERATURE %BHP	KTAS	GPH	20°C ABOVE STANDARD TEMP %BHP	KTAS	GPH
2000	2400	---	---	---	75	101	6.1	70	101	5.7
	2300	71	97	5.7	66	96	5.4	63	95	5.1
	2200	62	92	5.1	59	91	4.8	56	90	4.6
	2100	55	87	4.5	53	86	4.3	51	85	4.2
	2000	49	81	4.1	47	80	3.9	46	79	3.8
4000	2450	-	-	---	75	103	6.1	70	102	5.7
	2400	76	102	6.1	71	101	5.7	67	100	5.4
	2300	67	96	5.4	63	95	5.1	60	95	1
	2200	60	91	4.8	56	90	4.6	54	89	
	2100	53	86	4.4	51	85	4.2	49	84	4.0
	2000	48	81	3.9	46	80	3.8	45	78	3.7
6000	2500	---	- -	-	75	105	6.1	71	104	5.7
	2400	72	101	5.8	67	100	5.4	64	99	5.2
	2300	64	96	5.2	60	95	4.9	57	94	4.7
	2200	57	90	4.6	54	89	4.4	52	88	4.3
	2100	51	85	4.2	49	84	4.0	48	83	3.9
	2000	46	80	3.8	45	79	3.7	44	77	3.6
8000	2550	-	-		75	107	6.1	71	106	5.7
	2500	76	105	6.2	71	104	5.8	67	103	5.4
	2400	68	100	5.5	64	99	5.2	61	98	4.9
	2300	61	95	5.0	58	94	4.7	55	93	4.5
	2200	55	90	4.5	52	89	4.3	51	87	4.2
	2100	49	84	4.1	48	83	3.9	46	82	3.8
10,000	2500	72	105	5.8	68	103	5.5	64	103	5.2
	2400	65	99	5.3	61	98	5.C	58	97	4.8
	2300	58	94	4.7	56	93	4.5	53	92	4.4
	2200	53	89	4.3	51	88	4.2	49	86	4.0
	2100	48	83	4.0	46	82	3.9	45	81	3.8
12,000	2450	65	101	5.3	62	100	5.0	59	99	4.8
	2400	62	99	5.0	59	97	4.8	56	96	4.6
	2300	56	93	4.6	54	92	4.4	52	91	4.3
	2200	51	88	4.2	49	87	4.1	48	85	4.0
	2100	47	82	3.9	45	81	3.8	44	79	1 3.7

Fuel Planning Worksheet

Date: / /	Reg.

Cessna 152

		LITRES
ENROUTE TIME @ 25 LITRES / HOUR		37.5
10 % CONTINGENCY FUEL		3.8
RESERVE (45 MINS) @ 25 LITRES / HOUR		19
TAXI / TAKEOFF		3
UNUSABLE FUEL		6
	MIN FUEL REQUIRED	69.3
	TOTAL FUEL DIPPED	70
LESS UNUSABLE FUEL	(Included in aircraft empty weight)	-6
		63
LITRES TO POUNDS	(At a Specific Gravity of 0.72)	x 1.584
TOTAL FUEL WEIGHT TO WEIGHT AND BALANCE SHEET		100

Weight and Balance

The maximum takeoff and landing weight is 1670 pounds (758 kg).
The basic empty weight is approximately 1170 lbs (530 kg) and includes full oil and usable fuel. The actual basic weight figure of the aircraft you are flying must always be used for weight and balance calculations. Refer to the relevant weight and balance certificate (which should be not older then 5 years), which is found with the aircraft documents on board the aircraft, for exact weight of the aircraft you are flying.

Weight and balance documentation is not normally required for private flights, however it is still the pilot in command's responsibility to ensure that the aircraft is properly loaded and within limits. It is vital for safety and performance considerations to know your exact operating weight and condition before each take-off.

Minor overloading, or mis-loading, may not result in obvious structural damage, but can cause fatigue on internal structural components or produce hazardous aeroplane handling characteristics. Severe overloading can cause structural damage or loss of control due to adverse aerodynamic characteristics.

An overweight aircraft will have increased takeoff distance, climb rates, and landing distance. An overweight aircraft also has an increased stall speed, and where performance is critical this reduces the safe operating envelope and any manoeuvring which increases the loading can result in an inadvertent stall.

Aeroplane balance is maintained by controlling the position of the centre of gravity through correct loading. The centre of gravity must be within limits, as adverse balance moments will make the aircraft difficult to control, and loading outside Centre of Gravity limits can make the aircraft uncontrollable.
An aeroplane loaded past the rear limit of its permissible centre of gravity range will have an increased tendency for over-rotation, loss of elevator control on landing and, although a lower stall speed, a more unstable stall spin tendency.
Aircraft loaded past the forward limit will result in a higher stall speed, and a nose heavy moment, resulting in difficulty in rotation and flare, and a dangerous tendency for nose wheel landings or wheel-barrowing on takeoff and landing.

Weight and Balance Calculation

Once the weight of the minimum fuel required is known, the weight and balance requirements may be calculated.

Begin with entering the Aircraft Empty Weight. This may be obtained from the aircraft flight manual or documents folder and is different for every aeroplane. In this example we use a Basic Empty Weight figure of 1136 and Moment of 34000 lbs-ins.

Enter the actual weights or standard weights for the crew and passenger. If weights are not known standard weights must be used for all occupants. Then enter the fuel and baggage.
Add all the figures together to obtain the total takeoff weight. This must be less than the maximum allowable take off weight, 1670lbs. Should it be higher, weight must be removed until it is below the maximum. Baggage or passengers may be offloaded, or a shorter flight planned with a lower fuel requirement.

Moments may then be calculated by multiplying each of the weights (mass in lbs) by the respective moment arm (inches from the datum), to obtain the moment in lbs/inches. The total moment for takeoff and landing, are obtained by adding together all the individual moments.

NOTE: All weights and arms used in weight and balance calculation should be in the same units. Moments are divided by 1000 for more easily workable numbers, and this is also the format used in the Pilot's Operating Handbook.

Weight & Balance Worksheet

ITEM	WEIGHT			ARM	MOMENT / 1000				
Aircraft Empty Weight (Flt. Man)	1	1	3	6		3	4	.	0	0
Pilot		1	7	0	39		6	.	6	3
Passenger		1	5	0	39		5	.	8	5
Baggage Area 1 (Max 120 lbs)			2	0	64		1	.	2	8
Baggage Area 2 (Max 40 lbs)					84					
Fuel Weight (Max 147 lbs)		1	0	0	42		4	.	2	0
Takeoff Weight (Max 1600 lbs)	1	5	7	6	**32.96**	5	1	.	9	6
Less Fuel Burn			6	0	42		2	.	5	2
Landing Weight (Max 1600 lbs)	1	5	1	6	**32.61**	4	9	.	4	4

Weight x Arm = Moment. Centre of Gravity = Total Moments ÷ Total Weights

The centre of gravity of the aircraft in its takeoff condition can be determined by dividing the takeoff moment by takeoff weight. In our case the centre of gravity for takeoff will be 32.96 inches.

To determine that the centre of gravity is within the approved envelope, enter takeoff weight and position of the centre of gravity in the Centre of Gravity Limits graph from the POH, as shown in the example graph following.
If centre of gravity is located outside the envelope, the baggage should be shifted or removed and the weight and balance must be computed again to insure the aircraft centre of gravity located within the limit.
The landing condition may then be determined in similar manner, namely subtracting the fuel weight and moment from the takeoff figures and dividing the total landing moment by the total landing weight, to obtain a landing centre of gravity of 32.61 inches aft of the datum.

Some centre of gravity graphs display 'moment envelopes', that is, weight versus moment, in this case only the moment needs to be entered on the graph, however it is a good idea to calculate the position of the centre of gravity as a cross check on calculations.

CENTER OF GRAVITY LIMITS

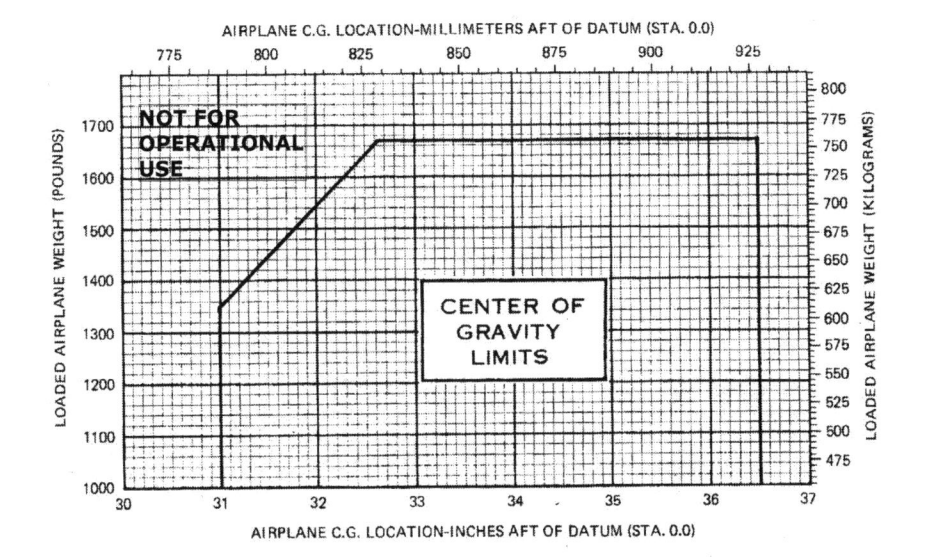

(chart: Airplane C.G. Location vs Loaded Airplane Weight, with "NOT FOR OPERATIONAL USE" marked)

It sometimes may be necessary to calculate how far we can fly with the load on board then plan fuel stops in the required distance, in this case the calculation must be reversed.

Take-off and Landing Performance Planning

Once we know what the actual weight will be for takeoff and landing, the takeoff and landing performance can be checked to ensure the field length is adequate. For this the tables takeoff distance and landing distance from the C152 POH must be used, these have been reproduced in the examples below.

In our example we will use the following conditions: 30°C ambient temperature, QNH 1005 and 5570' airfield elevation. No wind is considered, as an into wind runway should normally be chosen, increasing the performance and providing a safety buffer over the distance calculated. On one-way strips a tailwind if prevalent must be considered, up to the maximum limit of 10kts.

The pressure altitude was calculated using the standard formulas provided in the front of this manual. Remember all figures should be rounded up for safety margins, and make sure that all factors, such as runway slope and grass runway surface have been considered and applied correctly in the distances calculation.

The tables used in this example use pressure altitude and temperature, providing for density. In some POH's figures are only given for standard temperature at different altitudes, in this case you will need to calculate density altitude first. In our example below the difference is over 3000ft, which is quite significant to performance.

When reviewing the runway distance available, ensure length is considered in the correct units, if needed convert from feet to meters. The runway length available should be equal or greater than takeoff or landing distance required, whichever is higher.

Takeoff Performance

DEPARTURE AIRFIELD	WINDHOEK, EROS	DESIGNATOR	FYWE
VARIATION	14	AMBIENT TEMPERATURE	30
I.S.A.	1013		-15
LESS QNH	1005	+PRESS ALT/1000X2	11.6
DIFFERENCE	8	DIFF FROM STD TEMP	26.6
	x 30 feet		x 120 feet
	240		3192
PLUS ELEVATION	5570	PLUS PRESS ALT	5810
=PRESSURE ALTITUDE	5810	=DENSITY ALTITUDE	9002
WIND TRUE		+/- VAR	14	=WIND MAG	
		RUNWAY HEADING	
		ANGULAR DIFFERENCE	
CROSS WIND COMPONENT		HEADWIND COMPONENT	
MAX DEMONSTRATED			
		SLOPE	NIL SIG
		SURFACE	PAVED
		TAKE OFF ROLL REQUIRED	1455FT
		TOTAL TAKEOFF DISTANCE REQUIRED	2855FT
		TAKEOFF DISTANCE AVAILABLE	6000FT

TAKEOFF DISTANCE
SHORT FIELD

NOT FOR OPERATIONAL USE

CONDITIONS:
Flaps 10°
Full Throttle Prior to Brake Release
Paved, Level, Dry Runway
Zero Wind

NOTES:

1. Short field technique as specified in Section 4.
2. Prior to takeoff from fields above 3000 feet elevation, the mixture should be leaned to give maximum RPM in a full throttle, static runup.
3. Decrease distances 10% for each 9 knots headwind. For operation with tailwinds up to 10 knots, increase distances by 10% for each 2 knots.
4. For operation on a dry, grass runway, increase distances by 15% of the "ground roll" figure.

WEIGHT LBS	TAKEOFF SPEED KIAS LIFT OFF	TAKEOFF SPEED KIAS AT 50 FT	PRESS ALT FT	0°C GRND ROLL	0°C TOTAL TO CLEAR 50 FT OBS	10°C GRND ROLL	10°C TOTAL TO CLEAR 50 FT OBS	20°C GRND ROLL	20°C TOTAL TO CLEAR 50 FT OBS	30°C GRND ROLL	30°C TOTAL TO CLEAR 50 FT OBS	40°C GRND ROLL	40°C TOTAL TO CLEAR 50 FT OBS
1670	50	54	S.L.	640	1190	695	1290	755	1390	810	1495	875	1605
			1000	705	1310	765	1420	825	1530	890	1645	960	1770
			2000	775	1445	840	1565	910	1690	980	1820	1055	1960
			3000	855	1600	925	1730	1000	1870	1080	2020	1165	2185
			4000	940	1775	1020	1920	1100	2080	1190	2250	1285	2440
			5000	1040	1970	1125	2140	1215	2320	1315	2525	1420	2750
			6000	1145	2200	1245	2395	1345	2610	1455	2855	1570	3125
			7000	1270	2470	1375	2705	1490	2960	1615	3255	1745	3590
			8000	1405	2800	1525	3080	1655	3395	1795	3765	1940	4195

by D. Bruckert & O. Roud © 2004

Landing Performance

ARRIVAL AIRFIELD	WINDHOEK, EROS	DESIGNATOR	FYWE
VARIATION	14	AMBIENT TEMPERATURE	30
I.S.A.	1013		-15
LESS QNH	1005	+PRESS ALT/1000X2	11.6
DIFFERENCE	8	DIFF FROM STD TEMP	26.6
	x 30 feet		x 120 feet
	240		3192
PLUS ELEVATION	5570	PLUS PRESS ALT	5810
=PRESSURE ALTITUDE	5810	=DENSITY ALTITUDE	9002
WIND TRUE	+/- VAR	14 =WIND MAG	
		RUNWAY HEADING	
		ANGULAR DIFFERENCE	
CROSS WIND COMPONENT		HEADWIND COMPONENT	
MAX DEMONSTRATED			
		SLOPE	NIL SIG
	SURFACE	PAVED	

LANDING DISTANCE REQUIRED 2855FT
LANDING DISTANCE AVAILABLE 6000FT

LANDING DISTANCE

SHORT FIELD

CONDITIONS:
Flaps 30°
Power Off
Maximum Braking
Paved, Level, Dry Runway
Zero Wind

NOT FOR OPERATIONAL USE

NOTES:
1. Short field technique as specified in Section 4.
2. Decrease distances 10% for each 9 knots headwind. For operation with tailwinds up to 10 knots, increase distances by 10% for each 2 knots.
3. For operation on a dry, grass runway, increase distances by 45% of the "ground roll" figure.

WEIGHT LBS	SPEED AT 50 FT KIAS	PRESS ALT FT	0°C GRND ROLL	0°C TOTAL TO CLEAR 50 FT OBS	10°C GRND ROLL	10°C TOTAL TO CLEAR 50 FT OBS	20°C GRND ROLL	20°C TOTAL TO CLEAR 50 FT OBS	30°C GRND ROLL	30°C TOTAL TO CLEAR 50 FT OBS	40°C GRND ROLL	40°C TOTAL TO CLEAR 50 FT OBS
1670	54	S.L.	450	1160	465	1185	485	1215	500	1240	515	1265
		1000	465	1185	485	1215	500	1240	520	1270	535	1295
		2000	485	1215	500	1240	520	1270	535	1300	555	1330
		3000	500	1240	520	1275	540	1305	560	1335	575	1360
		4000	520	1275	540	1305	560	1335	580	1370	600	1400
		5000	540	1305	560	1335	580	1370	600	1400	620	1435
		6000	560	1340	580	1370	605	1410	625	1440	645	1475
		7000	585	1375	605	1410	625	1440	650	1480	670	1515
		8000	605	1410	630	1450	650	1480	675	1520	695	1555

by D. Bruckert & O. Roud © 2004

REVIEW QUESTIONS

1. If the magneto selector is turned to OFF:
a) there will be a drop in engine rpm;
b) the rpm will stay the same;
c) the engine will stop

2. Two separate ignition systems provide:
a) more safety only;
b) more efficient burning only;
c) more safety and more efficient burning;
d) dual position key switching.

3. Switching the ignition OFF connects the magneto system to ground:
a) true;
b) false.

4. If a magneto ground wire comes loose in flight, the engine:
a) will stop;
b) will continue running with lower rpm;
c) will continue running.

5. The spark plugs are provided with electrical supply from:
a) battery at all times;
b) the magnetos;
c) the battery at start-up and then the magnetos.

6. The most probable reason an engine continues to run after ignition switch has been turned off is:
a) carbon deposit glowing on the spark plugs;
b) a magneto ground wire is in contact with the engine casing;
c) a broken magneto ground wire.

7. Cessna 152 engine has:
a) fuel injection system;
b) carburettor located on the bottom of the engine;
c) carburettor located on the top of the engine.

8. Cessna 152 engines are:
a) affected by carburettor ice;
b) not affected by carburettor ice;

9. Carb. Heat is used to:
a) prevent carburettor ice;
b) provide better fuel mixing in the carburettor as it evaporates quickly;
c) to heat the air/fuel mixture, so to provide better air/fuel mixture burning in the engine.

10. The pilot controls the fuel/air ratio with the:
a) throttle;
b) carb heat;
c) mixture.

11. For takeoff at a sea level airport, the mixture control should be:
a) in the leaned position for maximum rpm;
b) in the full rich position;
c) the engine is not affected by mixture setting below 3000ft.

12. What will occur if no leaning is made with the mixture control as the flight altitude increases:
a) the volume of air entering the carburettor decreases and the amount of fuel decreases, resulting in a rich mixture;
b) the density of air entering the carburettor decreases and the amount of fuel increases, resulting in a rich mixture;
c) the density of air entering the carburettor decreases and the amount of fuel remains constant, resulting in a rich mixture.

13. The correct procedure to achieve the best fuel/air mixture when cruising at altitude is:
a) to move the mixture control toward LEAN until engine rpm starts to drop;
b) to move the mixture control toward LEAN until engine rpm reaches a peak value;
c) to move the mixture control toward RICH until engine rpm starts to drop;
d) to move the mixture control toward LEAN until engine rpm reaches a peak EGT and then toward RICH to get EGT 25-50°F below the peak.

14. Extra fuel in a rich mixture causes:
a) engine heating;
b) engine cooling;
c) does not affect the heating or cooling of the engine.

15. If after the mixture is properly adjusted at cruise at the altitude, pilot forgets to enrich the mixture during descent:
a) the engine may cut-out due to too rich mixture;
b) the engine may cut-out due to too lean mixture;
c) a too rich mixture will create high cylinder head temperatures;
d) a to lean mixture will create high cylinder head temperatures.

16. The remedy for suspected carburettor ice is to:
a) enrichen the mixture;
b) lean the mixture;
c) apply carb. heat;
d) increase power by advancing the throttle.

17. If carb. heat is applied:
a) rpm will increase due to the leaner mixture;
b) rpm will decrease due to the leaner mixture;
c) rpm will decrease due to the richer mixture.

18. When the engine is primed for start-up, the fuel priming pump delivers fuel:
a) through the carburettor to the induction manifold;
b) through the carburettor to each cylinder;
c) directly to the cylinders bypassing the carburettor.

19. When the engine is primed for start-up, the fuel priming pump delivers fuel:
a) through the carburettor to the induction manifold;
b) through the carburettor to each cylinder;
c) directly to the cylinders bypassing the carburettor.

20. Water tends to collect at the:
a) lowest point in the fuel system;
b) highest point in the fuel system

21. The engine oil system is provided to:
a) reduce friction between moving parts and ensure high engine temperatures;
b) reduce friction between moving parts and prevent high engine temperatures;
c) increase friction between moving parts and prevent high engine temperatures.

22. The engine oil system is provided to:
a) reduce friction between moving parts and ensure high engine temperatures;
b) reduce friction between moving parts and prevent high engine temperatures;
c) increase friction between moving parts and prevent high engine temperatures.

23. Oil grades:
a) should not be mixed;
b) may be mixed.

24. With too little oil, you may observe:
a) high oil temperature and high oil pressure;
b) high oil temperature and low oil pressure;
c) low oil temperature and low oil pressure.

25. What action can a pilot take to aid in cooling an engine that is overheating during a climb:
a) lean the mixture and increase airspeed;
b) enrichen the mixture and increase airspeed;
c) increase airspeed and reduce engine rpm.

26. Normal in-flight electrical power is provided by an:
a) alternator;
b) battery;
c) generator.

27. A distribution point for electrical power to various services is:
a) circuit breaker;
b) distributor;
c) bus bar.

28. The battery master switch should be turned to OFF after the engine is stopped to avoid the battery discharging through:
a) the magnetos;
b) the generator;
c) electrical services connected to it.

29. The suction (or vacuum gauge) shows the pressure:
a) below atmospheric pressure;
b) above atmospheric pressure.

30. The suction (or vacuum gauge) shows the pressure:
a) below atmospheric pressure;
b) above atmospheric pressure.

31. The vacuum pump is:
a) electrically-driven;
b) engine-driven;
c) hydraulically-driven.

32. The following instrument will be affected by a vacuum pump failure:
a) artificial horizon and the direction indicator;
b) turn and bank indicator;
c) airspeed indicator.

33. The pilot should shut-down an engine after start if the oil pressure does not rise within:
a) 30 seconds;
b) 1 minute;
c) 10 seconds.

34. The aircraft is equipped with:
a) a fixed pitch propeller;
b) a constant speed propeller.

35. The aircraft is equipped with:
a) a fixed pitch propeller;
b) a constant speed propeller.

36. Engine power is monitored by the:
a) manifold pressure gauge;
b) engine rpm gauge.

37. The usual method of shutting an engine down is to:
a) switch the magnetos off;
b) move the mixture to idle cut-off;
c) switch the master switch off.

38. The usual method of shutting an engine down is to:
a) switch the magnetos off;
b) move the mixture to idle cut-off;
c) switch the master switch off.

39. The minimum oil quantity for takeoff is:
a) 3 quarts;
b) 4 quarts;
c) 5 quarts;
d) 6 quarts

40. Fuel tanks is are located:
a) in the aft cabin;
b) beneath the pilot seats;
c) in the wings.

41. The aircraft is equipped with:
a) electrically operated elevator trim tab;
b) manually-operated elevator trim;
c) manually-operated elevator and rudder trim.

42. Frise type ailerons are used to:
a) reduce airflow over the control surface to make the control lighter;
b) reduce the adverse aileron yaw during bank;
c) this aircraft does not have Frise type of ailerons.

43. The flaps are:
a) hydraulically-operated;
b) electrically-operated;
c) manually-operated.

44. Flaps selections are:
a) 10, 20 and 30 degrees;
b) take-off, approach and land;
c) 15, 30 and 45 degrees

45. Nose wheel steering is provided by:
a) mechanical links with rudder pedals;
b) differential braking;
c) all of the above.

Fill in the following from the aircraft you are flying:

Aircraft model _____, year _____;

46. The best glide speed at maximum weight is _____.

47. The best rate of climb speed at sea level is_____, at 10'000ft_____.

48. The recommended normal climb speed at sea level is_____.

49. The recommended takeoff speed at sea level, and maximum weight for a short field is_____, for a normal landing is_____.

50. The recommended landing speed at sea level and maximum weight for a short field is_____, for a normal landing is_____.

Made in the USA
Columbia, SC
24 February 2019